THE GERMAN STRUGGLE AGAINST YUGOSLAV GUERRILLAS IN WORLD WAR II

GERMAN COUNTER-INSURGENCY IN YUGOSLAVIA 1941-1943

by
PAUL N. HEHN

EAST EUROPEAN QUARTERLY, BOULDER
DISTRIBUTED BY COLUMBIA UNIVERSITY PRESS
NEW YORK

1979

EAST EUROPEAN MONOGRAPHS, NO. LVII

Paul N. Hehn is Associate Professor of History
at the State University College at Brockport

To My Wife Pat—To Whom I Owe Everything

CONTENTS

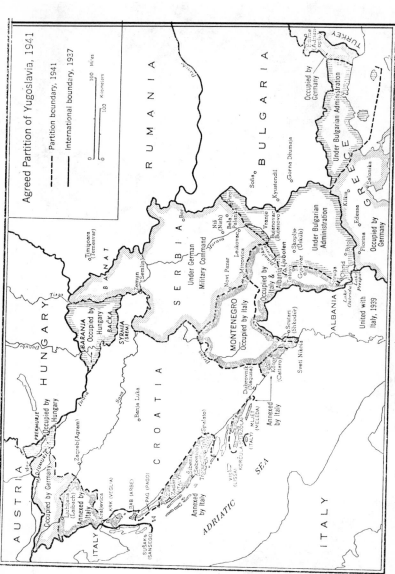

Source: *Documents on German Foreign Policy 1918-1945*, D, XII

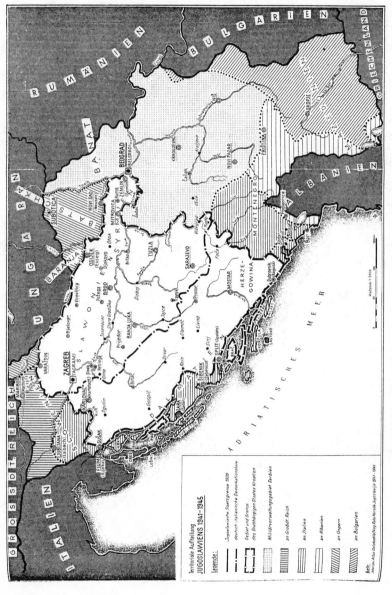

Source: *Jstoriski Atlas Oslobodilačkog Rata Naroda Jugoslavije 1941–1945*

INTRODUCTION

The guerrilla war inside the former Yugoslav state during the years 1941-1945 was, from every standpoint—military, political, psychological—a unique conflict with many dimensions. Outwardly it was a struggle against German and Italian fascism and its domestic retainers and in this sense it was a part of the general international conflagration of World War II. Within the struggle against the German and Italian armies that occupied Yugoslavia after its collapse in April 1941 raged a civil war and revolutionary confrontation between the communist-led partisans and their nationalist rivals the Serbian *četnik* and Croatian *ustasha* organizations.[1] This work views the conflict from the viewpoint of the German military and as such it is primarily a study of the military side of the war in the southeast with important insights into the political area. It is therefore a significant work in that it was commissioned by the German High Command and written by General Wisshaupt while the conflict was still going on. Hence it has the virtue of dramatic immediacy and captures the atmosphere and inner tension surrounding important decisions and problems which time tends to dampen.

While Berlin was not unaware of the ideological and political side of the struggle which surfaces from time to time in the present study, the savage social revolution that was being fought out was secondary to the overall German objective of crushing the resistance and restoring control over the region. For the German High Command and Hitler both the partisans and četniks, regardless of their ideological antipathies, represented two sides of the same coin, i.e., a national uprising by the "Serb conspiratorial clique" against the occupiers and their supporters. Local German commanders, however, were often quick to establish distinctions between the contending guerrilla organizations, though some of the operational commanders like General Boehme, sent in to suppress the 1941 uprising in Serbia also shared the linear view of Hitler and the OKW. The latter even doubted the utility of using the various paramilitary organizations liked the Serbian Guard (*Srpska Straža*) and Volunteers (*Dobrovoljci*) against the guerrillas. To the end Hitler also believed that neither the latter nor the četniks were trustworthy and could not be supported or armed against the partisans or against one another. As late as 1944 he refused to grant the request of General Nedić, wartime leader of occupied Serbia, for guns to fight the partisans.[2]

The German High Command regarded the guerrilla movement in the southeast—somewhat simplistically— as an uprising (*Aufstand*) against the legally constituted authority. In this respect it perceived the struggle against the "rebels," "bandits," "insurgents," and "bands," as it referred to the guerrillas as a conflict with a small number of malcontents while the greater part of the population accepted or at least tolerated the occupation of their country by foreign forces. Like all occupiers they could not conceive of the disaffection for the occupation in the general population. They believed that the majority of the population was either neutral or favored the German-sponsored regimes of General Nedić in Serbia and the Ustasha regime in Croatia. Hence, they repeatedly used invidious references to the guerrillas as "insurgents" or "rebels." Only much later in the war the Germans dropped the use of the term "bands."

While local German and especially Italian field commanders drew distinctions between the četnik forces of Draza Mihailović and the partisans and continuously strove to play the two guerrilla forces against each other, Hitler and the German High Command regarded this as a dangerous game. It did not matter to them that the two guerrilla organizations had antagonistic ideological differences that could be beneficially exploited: the enemy whether nationalist or communist had to be smashed wherever he appeared. Thus a conflict developed between the local German field commanders who were inclined to employ the četniks against the partisans or to strike arrangements wherever possible to spare German blood and orders to avoid collaboration from OKW headquarters in Berlin. The Italians were less fastidious and more unscrupulous than the Germans and took quite another view of the matter. Having exacted as their price for the creation of the Independent State of Croatia under the crown of Italy, the Dalmatian coast and fortified areas in the interior in zones 2 and 3, Rome quickly became disenchanted with its creation when the Ustasha regime demonstrated pro-German sentiments and rejected Italian dictates. By the end of 1941 as the Germans became hard pressed in other theatres and saw no way of ending the deteriorating situation in Croatia created by the Ustasha's terror policy against the Serbian minority they seriously considered withdrawing completely from the Croatian area and turning it over to the Italians. But, dissuaded by the reports of the Croatophile military commander in

Croatia Glaise von Horstenau, the OKW changed its mind and decided to remain in Croatia.[3] The Italians virtually ceased fighting the četniks throughout the Independent Croatian State and began to enter into collaborative arrangements with them against the Ustasha regime. This development proved fatal. Italian cosseting of the četniks and their general disenchantment with the war in the southeast compromised the entire German effort to crush the guerillas without committing large numbers of their own troops. Without the Italian Second Army playing an active role, the Germans could do little against the partisans that was conclusive and the anti-guerilla front was broken.

During the second world war the German High Command considered the Balkan theatre to be a secondary war zone, a rear area which the German soldier preferred to the Russian or North African fronts, but less preferable to occupation duty in France and the Low Countries. But this conception quickly changed. General Rendulic, appointed in 1943 to crush the guerillas in Croatia, reported that after assuming his post over 1,000 German soldiers requested transfer to any other area, even the eastern front, rather than face the savage, no quarter battle conditions in the southeast.[4]

The mortality rate on the southeastern front was not high but neither was it negligible. One study of the southeastern theatre of war states that one out of seven soldiers in German uniform—whether German or not—became a casualty by the close of operations. It would be a mistake as some have alleged to assume that although the Germans could still march into Greece, Albania or Yugoslavia at will even in their most weakened condition, that the resistance movement had only a gadfly value.[5] Hitler and Mussolini were in constant communication on the guerilla movement in the southeast and it became a major bone of contention between the Axis High Commands.[6] Moreover, the necessity of deploying troops from other war zones at critical moments in the war, and the constantly impending danger of a stab in the back Allied invasion of the Balkans as in the Salonika front in the first world war, made it imperative for the German High Command to eliminate the guerilla movement.

There were also definite economic reasons for the German decision to remain in southeastern Europe, namely, for the bauxite, copper and lead mines of the Croatian and Serbian areas necessary for the German war economy. Foodstuffs and Turkish chrome shipped up the Balkan supply arteries to the Reich were also indispensable to the Germans. Even after the capture of Rome, the Germans were compelled to remain in the Balkans despite the danger of being outflanked out of sheer economic necessity. Approximately 50 per cent of Germany's oil, all of its chrome, 60 per cent of its bauxite, 24 per cent of its antimony and 21 per cent of its copper were procured from Balkan sources.[7] Vast supplies of war materials for Rommel's armies in Africa also passed down the Balkan railway route, besides the continuous flow of raw materials to Germany, any interruption of which would have had a serious effect upon the German war effort. Keeping these transportation arteries open at all times became one of the main tasks of the occupation. Apart from economic requirements, the Balkans also formed the covering flank for Germany's South Russian position and shielded southern and central Europe from Allied land forces. An Allied land assault in the Adriatic linking up the Yugoslav and Greek guerillas was a nightmare possibility that haunted the German High Command and Hitler. Such an undertaking could erode away Germany's East European satellites leaving a wide cleavage immediate before the eastern front and outflanking Germany's position in Russia from the southeast. It would also trap the Axis troops located in the Balkan region.

The situation in the southeast became unstable from the very start of the occupation following the collapse of Yugoslavia and Greece in April 1941. In the summer and autumn of 1941 revolts broke out in Serbia, Montenegro, Herzegovina, Bosnia and Croatia following the withdrawal of German troops to the eastern front. In the Independent State of Croatia the resistance flared up in the Serb-populated areas as a response to the massacres of large numbers of Serbs by the Ustasha. Additional complicating factors were the proclamation of an independent Montenegrin state linked to Italy through the behind the scenes connivance of the Italians and separatist "greens" (zelenaši) on July 12, 1941, followed by a revolt of the Montenegrin population in reaction the following day, and the entry of the Soviet Union into the war encouraging both communists and non-communists in the belief that the war had entered a new phase and the Axis would be defeated.[8] In Montenegro, led by the communists who were joined by many ex-royalist officers and nationalist-minded persons ashamed of the humiliating collapse of Yugoslavia's resistance several months earlier and simmering over the Italian occupation of their land, the revolt went far beyond the expectations of the communist leaders. The latter had only intended to start small guerrilla actions at first, but were carried along by the general exultation and hatred of the occupier.

In western Serbia after a short honeymoon of cooperation between Mihailović's četniks and the communist-led partisans against the Nedić regime, the resistance forces fell out and began fighting one another. Mihailović opposed attacking the enemy frontally from the outset, realizing that stronger enemy forces would immediately be rushed in and the guerrillas would be engulfed. This, in fact, occurred. At his post war trial in Yugoslavia, Mihailović testified somewhat condescendingly that the partisans "were amateurs in military science" and "the uprising was premature...the time had not come to fight the invader."[10] Orders from London to avoid a frontal clash with the enemy and the chastening effect of the German reprisal executions in Kragujevac and Kraljevo during the fall of 1941 decided him on a policy of waiting until German military strength ebbed or had been dealt a severe blow by the Allies before going over to the offensive. In the first attacks against the Germans the partisan forces were undoubtedly the most heavily engaged. Četnik units engaged in the fighting only at the end of August and in mid-September in the case of Major Dragoslav Račić who jointly invested Šabac with the partisans and Colonel Mišite at Loznice. At that point the partisan efforts aided by the četniks flared up into a full scale uprising in western Serbia. However, partisan historians claim that the cetniks entered the struggle only because they feared partisan successes would make Tito too strong and because they wanted to share in the booty.[11]

From the first the partisans adopted a policy of unremitting sruggle to drive the invader and his supporters out of the country regardless of costs, and their struggle took on the form of a national crusade. Within these liberationist objectives they openly avowed their aim of carrying out a social revolution.[12] Their scarcely concealed intentions of establishing a socialist state alarmed their Soviet benefactors who cautioned them against frightening the British and Americans and urged them to concentrate upon fighting the occupier and avoid alienating potential followers. This advice and the calamitous effects of a sectarian and dogmatic policy in Montenegro, Herzegovina, and Serbia which the četniks exploited and cost the partisans dearly in the support of the population, led them to modify their line and concentrate upon rallying all those who wished to fight the occupier and his supporters.[13]

The contest in the former Yugoslav state was from the start a national struggle against German and Italian fascism and its desire to convert the region into an economic dependency of the Axis. Before World War II Yugoslavia had been almost a colony of western European capital investment, primarily British and French capital, in much the same manner as Russia had been before 1914.[14] But from the 1930's on Germany began to challenge British and French entrenched capital, primarily through its encroachment into the Yugoslav export and import market. The Third Reich's need for assured sources of minerals and foodstuffs to feed its voracious war economy necessitated its playing a major role in the region despite disclaimers to the Italians that it had no interests in the Balkans.[15] What is, however, more important is that the struggle within international capitalism, i.e., between the British and French on the one hand and the Germans and Italians—and also, for that matter, between the two Axis partners as well—not only divided the western bourgeoisie in the capitalist world but also divided the national bourgeoisie inside Yugoslavia, a segment of which allied with Anglo-French capital interests and was opposed by another segment which sided with German and Italian fascism.[16]

With the rise of Fascism in the 1930's, particularly the emergence of the Hitler regime in Germany, the contradictions between the western capitalist powers had temporarily overshadowed their mutual hostility to the Soviet Union. A situation arose similar to the conflict between the imperialist nations of western Europe perceived by Lenin during the first world war weakening the capitalist world and permitting the Bolshevik Revolution to erupt. War as a means of extending Socialism into new areas was fully perceived by Stalin who told the Yugoslav leader Milovan Djilas that World War III would bring still more territories into the socialist system.[17]

Besides the conflict between the western powers and the Axis there were also serious imperialist rivalries within the Axis between the Italians and the Germans that prevented a consolidation of efforts against the guerrillas. The Italianophobe German commander in Croatia von Glaise-Horstenau complained of anti-German speeches by his Italian counterpart General Oxilia before Croat officers and of Italian toleration of the četniks in their occupation zone.[18] German-Italian frictions were not lost on Ante Pavelić, leader of the Ustasha regime, who commented laconically: "They are like cat and dog."[19] The Germans also jealously complained that the Italians were draining Croatia's wealth: "Dalmatia," Glaise remarked, "could very well become an Italian suction pump for the Croatian economy."[20] The maintenance of eleven to twelve Italian divisions was also a severe strain on the Croatian economy.

Besides the frictions between the Axis powers there were also incessant sub-rivalries between the Italians and the Croatian Ustasha regime. Italian abettment of četnik attacks upon the Croatian and Moslem population in their occupation zone from which the četniks sallied into the German zone also irritated both the Germans and Croatian government.[21] The ineptitude of the Croatian army, built from the ground up by the Croatian leader, Marshal Kvaternik, in dealing with the partisans and četniks caused a seepage of support for the Ustasha regime in Croatia. A German agent travelling through Banja Luka reported that food shortages and the inability of the Ustasha regime to deal with the guerrillas, had shaken the confidence of the public which "looks to any force that can bring order out of chaos whether Italian or četnik."[22] In a word, all these intense rivalries and insurmountable problems between the Axis powers and their allies were hardly conducive to the conduct of a common anti-guerrilla campaign and in the end the failure to weld together a united front proved fatal to the entire war effort in the southeast. The pursuit of a unified front against the partisans and the failure to achieve it was the continuing central preoccupation of the German High Command.

As mentioned, the pre-war conflict between the Axis and the western European liberal capitalist regimes had fatal repercussions within the national bourgeoisie in Yugoslavia. Even before the outbreak of the war in Europe serious antagonisms developed between the Croatian and Serbian bourgeoisies, the former represented by the Croatian Peasant Party led by Stepan Radić and later Vladko Maček and the latter by Nikola Pašić and in the mid-1930's by Milan Stojadinović. The more conservative segments of the Serbian bourgeoisie, following the collapse of Yugoslavia in April 1941, like Dimitrje Ljotic and his ultra-rightist Zbor movement and the former war minister General Milan Nedić collaborated with the occupation regime. Similarly, the Ustasha regime in the Independent State of Croatia also adopted a corporatist, pro-Axis posture. Despite their common hostility to the western parliamentary regimes, the mutual national hostilities between the two pro-fascist regimes in Serbia and Croatia made them irreconcilable enemies and created indissoluble barriers to a unified anti-guerrilla front.

The political groups associated with the pre-war parliamentary regime like the Croatian Peasant Party either remained quiescent or ceased to exercise any influence during the war primarily because of pre-war political corruption and the ignominious military collapse of the Yugoslav state. At the same time, the dominant pre-war political parties and social class feared the National Liberation Movement and its social revolutionary aims more than Hitler. In Serbia these uprooted elements of the national bourgeoisie regrouped around the Serb officers of the old army under Colonel Draža Mihailović. The latter had been associated with the March 27, 1941 coup of disaffected Serbian officers against the government of Dragiša Cvetković for signing the Tripartite Treaty with the Axis.[23] Mihailović had been connected to the group of Serb officers around General Bora Mirković and British intelligence, the SOE organization, whish, as one writer states, "may explain the later British commitment to Mihailovic."[24] The četnik organization based itself in Serbia and the Serb-populated areas of the west and south and upon the more affluent peasantry and petty officialdom in the villages and towns. The Croatian bourgeoisie centered around the powerful pre-war Croatian Peasant Party and refused to associate itself either with the Great Serbia-oriented četnik movement, the fascist ustasha party or the partisan movement. With the incarceration of its leader, Maček, throughout the war by the ustasha regime, it assumed a mugwump position which caused its disintegration and decline in influence. Except for some Croat intellectuals and a few Croatian units from Dalmatia and Slavonia which joined the partisans, the Croats for the most part did not participate in any of the resistance groups.[25]

The massacres of Serbs in the Independent State of Croatia by the ustasha and četnik counterattacks upon the Croatian and Moslem population split and fragmented the national bourgeoisie and further weakened and compromised the class that had formerly dominated the country. National hatred of the occupiers and their servitors enabled the partisans to mobilize the beggarized masses in the rural areas and towns and villages and convert the popular struggle into a social revolution.

At first the partisan leaders tried to form a united front with the cetniks against the occupation, but after initial cooperation Mihailović broke with the partisans in early November 1941. From this point on the guerrilla anti-fascist front was broken. Some of Mihailović's lieutenants drifted into compromising relationships with the occupation forces either with the Nedić forces, occasionally the Ustasha or with the Italians in the western regions. At any rate četnik attempts to run with both the hares and the hounds resulted in disaster for the movement in the long run.[26]

The picture that emerges from the German view of the war in the southeast was that of a tenacious and resourceful guerrilla foe who neither gave nor expected any quarter. The perils and frustrations of the East Bosnian campaign where the enemy demonstrated an ability to employ to advantage terrain, weather and demography are graphically described by a German commander in the field.

> There were many surprises, miserable snowed up mule tracks, infernal cold always between 30 and 40 degrees. We could not take over any billets because there were no localities which sufficed and because many houses had been burned down.
>
> The operation in mid-winter had to drive the Communists from their positions in the hills and disperse them. This was accomplished. The majority of the enemy however retreated into the woods and some of them had probably wandered away to the south into the Italian zone. . . . It is quite impossible especially at this time of the year in knee deep snow, to mop up these people. It is not even possible in summer however improbable that may seem. It is an extremely broken up, rocky terrain, with perpendicular rock faces, deep gorges, gigantic forests. Considering the wonderful signals system of the bands whose spies lie in wait somewhere among the rocks, under a bush or at the edge of the forest, it is impossible to draw near without camouflage. When I was in Rogatice, it was reported to me that a unit of about 100 Communists was situated in a locality in the neighborhood. On the previous day, a patrol had been fired on from the heights above this village. I therefore ordered my battalion to surround the village at a distance at night. Before dawn penetration was made from all sides. The whole band, approximately 100 men, was destroyed. However, such operations are only successful at night. I needed the whole battalion to clear this village!

Similar, even more definitive conclusions were reached on the impossibility of stifling the guerilla movement:

> Even though our troops carried out their mission bravely, the planned encirclement and the complete destruction of the enemy in such an extensive area between the Drina-Bosna and Preća was not achieved. As in the previous fights with the bands, so in those winter days they accomplished praiseworthy results. In violent cold and driving snow, they marched along wretched roads covered with ice and along mule tracks, and had to fight a malicious enemy who could not be caught, in a wild mountainous country. *The guerrillas were everywhere and nowehere. It was possible to disperse them, but not to destroy them completely. They defended themselves in their position in the rocks, and then quickly dispersed again into their villages, where they acted like "peaceful" peasants in a "friendly" manner towards our troops.*

The partisans displayed the same fierce determination during the German campaign against them in the Kozara mountains of West Bosnia. Here the combined German and Croatian forces encountered

> a tenacious and well armed adversary who knew how to defend him-
> self cleverly in his mountain positions on the edges of steep defiles
> and frequently went over to counterattacks. Even women took part
> in the fight. When the 1st Croatian mountain division, carelessly and
> unprepared, collided with this strong enemy on the western edge of
> the Kozara, its front broke up. On the 21st the 2nd Croatian brigade
> suffered another heavy reverse. On the next day, the 22nd, the insur-
> gents advanced on the northern flank of the Croatians and threw
> back the 1st Croatian mountain brigade too acrosss the Bos. Dubica-
> Prijedor highway as far as 10 km. southwest of Bos.Dubica.

What accounts for the ability of the partisans to survive the repeated campaigns of the Axis forces to eliminate them? Undoubtedly, the mountainous terrain and dense forests of the region were particularly suitable for guerilla warfare. However, other areas in Eastern Europe and elsewhere with the same advantages in terrain and topography fail-ed to produce resistance movements during the second world war. One explanation lies in the traditions and fierce individualism of south Slavic society. In many parts of the country clan traditions and feudal survivals still persisted, particularly in the more inaccessible regions of Monte-negro, Bosnia and Herzegovina among the more primitive elements of the Orthodox Serbian peasantry. It was the latter whom the Ustasha massacres and religious persecutions drove en masse into the ranks of the guerrillas.[27] Berlin's support of the Ustasha regime in Croatia and German reprisal executions in Serbia caused many Serbs to join the guerillas. Rumors circulated that the Germans were behind the Ustasha attacks on the Serbs. Thus, the guerilla forces were almost exclusively composed of Orthodox Serbs, often survivors of Ustasha attacks upon families and relatives who had been expelled from their homes.

The calamitious effects of these unbridled attacks upon the Serbian population inside the Croatian state are described in graphic terms.

> After the unparalled collapse of the Yugoslav State the insurgent
> movement which flared up shortly after the outbreak of the German-
> Russian war, found a fertile breeding ground in the actions of the
> surrounding states. From the territory between the Theiss and the
> Danube which had been turned over to Hungary, more than 37,000
> Serbs, about 100,000 from Croatia and 20,000 from Bulgarian
> Macedonia were expelled into the remaining Serbian territory, all
> without any belongings in the most abject misery. These hordes of
> refugees had in many cases been witnesses to the murder of their de-
> pendents. They had nothing more to lose. With their sudden influx
> into Old Serbia, they could neither be placed or billeted anywhere.
> Therefore, they allied themselves by the thousands to the bands.

The centuries old Balkan tradition of guerrilla warfare and banditry as a way of gaining justice from a tyrannical social system was but a short step to the expression of popular indignation through an uprising to drive out a foreign occupier. The hasty departure of the Germans after the end of the Balkan campaign for the Russian front reduced German forces to a skeletal occupation force insufficient to cope with any large scale uprising. Many former Serbian officers and their men had avoided surrender and internment and fled into the forests awaiting the moment when they might fight again. An additionally important factor was the wounded national pride of the Serbs who had now fallen to their lowest point since Turkish times, which found expression in the patriotic appeal of the *ustanak* now summoned forth by the guerrilla movement. The contemptuous racial attitude and treatment of the South Slavs by Nazi SS officials added grist to this mill.

None of these things completely explain the ability of the partisans to maintain themselves against hopeless odds and a better equipped, numerically superior foe. One undoubted explanation is the organizing ability and leadership of the Communist Party which, from the arrival of instructions from the Comintern in Moscow, unleased a guerrilla war against the occupiers that took the form of a national crusade.

Ironically, at the end of the 1930's the Yugoslav Communist Party had become so faction-ridden that the Comintern had considered dissolving it. But under Tito's leadership by the Fourth Party Congress it had become a united and formidable party. Even before the guerrilla campaign had begun, following the collapse of the Yugoslav state in April 1941, the communists had organized a number of detachments, though they did not react to mount organized resistance before June 22, 1941.[28] The recruits that made up the partisan forces during the fighting in western Serbia in the fall of 1941 were in the main party members.[29] The party regulars became the nucleus around which newer recruits gathered, swelling the partisan ranks. Between the ideological conviction of the former and the nationalist fervor of the latter, the partisans composed a formidable military organization. The addition of many former royal Yugoslav army officers enhanced its operational capability. A report by Staatsrat Dr. Harald Turner, chief of the occupational administration attests to the frustrations of the Germans in trying to eradicate the guerrilla organization.

All our attempts to channel these people in a constructive direction
and separate them from the Communists have failed and had to be
abandoned. We have argued with them, conferred with them, cajol-
ed them and threatened them, but all to no purpose. We do not believe that it is possible to achieve anything in this country on the
basis of authority. The people just do not recognize authority. A minority question cannot be created among the Serbs as it was with
such success among the Croats. Practically nobody is interested in
the old political parties. They do not believe in anyone any more
and they follow the Communist bandits blindly. With their slogans
the Communists have succeeded in rallying around them elements,
that, in the past, would never have dreamt of cooperating with them.
Some go so far as to prefer Bolshevism to occupation by our troops—
and these are people on whose cooperation we were counting. Only
one means is left: armed force. It is difficult to get any sense [sic]
out of the Militia. The Italians are worse. Our intensified propaganda
to the effect that things are going badly for the Bolsheviks at the
front has proved useless. My impression is that even the news of the
capitulation of the Soviet Union would not cause these bandits to
capitulate. They are tougher than anything you can imagine. What is
more their organization is excellent. It might serve as the classic example of of a perfect secret organization.[30]

Similar reports on the difficulties of coping with the situation were
sent to Berlin by the Foreign Office representative, Dr. Benzler.

Rebels are being recruited from Communists, criminals in jails, bands
and from the countless destitute Serbian refugees from Croatia and
Hungary. The conspiratorial clique represents a national-Great Serbia
program and a Communist-Soviet program.

At the same time sharp attacks against the Communists and con-
spirators and therefore necessarily against the national Serbian intel-
ligenz will immediately lead to Serbian-Communist unity.

Existing German occupation troops and police are too weak to finish
the affair. The insurgent movement in Croatia and Montenegro as
well as communist influence from Bulgaria worsens the situation....
Discovery of the center of the conspiracy clique is very difficult as
traitors and work with money is rather without prospects. Veesen-
meyer's disguised Croatian helpers have achieved no palpable success.

Inflation, a numerous academic proletariat and the necessary reduc-
tion of the old Yugoslav administrative apparatus as well as the influx
of destitute refugees strengthens the communist danger. Loss of the
Banat to Hungary will increase the hopelessness and undermine the
authority and will to act of the Commissariat Government and pro-
mote the drift to Communism. Communist Fehmterror makes cooperation of loyal Serbs in the struggle against communism almost
impossible and makes things extremely difficult.... Countering it
can only be achieved after defeating of the communist terror and
through comprehensive mass arrests and expulsion of those arrested
to safe areas.[31]

These communications indicate that the partisans were the most aggressive of the two resistance organizations committed to a strategy of ceaseless struggle against the occupiers and their supporters at whatever the cost. However, the Germans remained fearful of the četnik organization with its predominantly Serbian officer leadership as the most dangerous of the two resistance groups. German reports perceived the četniks as possessing the requisite professional officer cadres capable of converting an uprising of loosely organized, irregular forces into a centralized, well-coordinated military organization. In addition the Germans believed that the Mihailović group could draw upon a greater mass base than the partisans, particularly among the chauvinist and royalist-oriented Serbian small landowners and petty bourgeoisie in the towns and villages. The latter, the Germans believed, would not be attracted to the partisan appeal of communism and social revolution, but rather to the traditionalism and nationalism of the četniks. As time passed these expectations failed to materialize. The more aggressive partisan group loomed as the main enemy despite the continued apprehensions about the Mihailović četniks by the German field commanders in their reports to Berlin. Mihailović's increasingly cautious and passive efforts against the Germans in Serbia, joint četnik actions with the Germans and Italians against the partisans in Bosnia and Herzegovina in 1942, and his continuing political and ideological preoccupations about the partisans as a more dangerous enemy than the Germans who would ultimately lose the war and depart from the Balkans, all began to exercize a fatal disintegrating influence upon the četnik organization and his own credibility in the eyes of the British. As a number of Mihailović's followers drifted into uneasy collaboration with the Italians and Germans and even the ustasha in Bosnia, Herzegovina, Montenegro and Slovenia, the British and Germans both began to discount his organization's effectiveness. Sporadic četnik campaigns and activity did not convince the Allied leaders and all military aid to Mihailović was curtailed. Mihailović's bad relations with the British worsened from 1943 onward until he was all but abandoned. Thus the German struggle against the guerilla forces after 1941-42 was less and less against the četniks and increasingly directed against the partisans.

An additional reason for the final victory of the partisans was undoubtedly the Yugoslav political orientation of the partisans as opposed to the Great Serbian and Great Croatian outlook of the četnik and ustasha movements. Attacks by the nationalist organizations—četniks against the Croats and Moslems, and the ustasha and sometimes the Moslems against the Orthodox population—had seriously compromised the narrower Great Serbian and Great Croatian nationalisms. The communists also had made similar mistakes in their indiscriminate use of terror, but succeeded in correcting them sufficiently to erase their earlier image as dogmatic and blindly sectarian visionaries. As the communist leaders perceived that the more the movement assumed a national stature the more they gained the popular support of the masses, the pragmatic fires of war slowly tempered their political maturation, forcing out the dross of dogmatism and sectarianism. The needs of nation and people temporarily took precedence over the ardently desired social transformation and the earlier overtly and stridently proclaimed social revolutionary goals became subsumed in the common struggle to defeat the enemy.

All this raises the pivotal question of whether the insurrection was primarily a national or a social revolt. In addition, the decisive role of the western powers and the Soviet Union must be thoroughly examined to ascertain the influences from abroad upon the guerilla movement. However, the relative equation between these vexing questions lies beyond the scope of this commentary.

The structure and purpose of the German occupation administration was ill-equipped to counter a revolt. The functions and powers of the military administrators and Nazi party political officials frequently overlapped, leading to constant jurisdictional problems that had to be referred to Berlin for settlement. Feuds and conflicts between high level officials were commonplace. Similar conflicts occurred between the operational field commanders like General Boehme and the military commanders at the head of regional and territorial administrations, the former being committed to operational and combat concerns while the latter were chiefly military administrators.

From the beginning the Germans grappled with the task of containing a formidable guerrilla enemy with the few reliable forces at their disposal. In fact, the Germans and Italians, together with their Croatian and Serbian allies, greatly outnumbered the partisans, but the political conflicts between them, the general unsuitability of the badly equpped and inept Croatian army, and Italian chicanery and passivity greatly reduced the effectiveness of the anti-guerrilla forces. Even before the opening of offensive operations in western Serbia in the fall of 1941 against the guerrillas, the German High Command in Serbia was aware of the difficulty—if not the impossibility—of eradicating the resistance given the paucity of men and equipment assigned to a secondary war theatre. It, therefore, considered a modus vivendi with the insurgents which would at the same time preserve its vital interests. General Foertsch suggested maintaining a "German corridor" betwen Belgrade-Niš-Skoplje and the Belgrade-Niš highway to Macedonia and Bulgaria. His rationale for this was explicit and practical:

> We do not wish to retain Serbia as part of the Reich and for that reason pacify it in the manner of the Protectorate or Poland. We want to take as much economic advantage as possible from the country. Above all, however, we want to safeguard communications between the Reich and the Balkans, provisions for economic trans-portation and for any deployment movements which become neces-sary. We cannot pacify the whole of Serbia at one time, i.e., destroy all the insurgents, we can only mop up a limited area. . . . Insurgents will have freedom of action in other areas southwest of the line. Only after limited mopping up in the corridor troops will be deploy-ed into the southwest area from the corridor base to attack the rebels in their bases.

In the end the German theatre commander rejected this proposal be-cause it gave the guerrillas too much freedom of action and meant the admission of a no-win strategy.[32] New campaigns to liquidate the guer-rilas were mounted and in the succeeding years specially trained moun-tain and anti-guerrilla units were brought in, but with the fall of Italy in 1943 and the influx of American and British supplies and equipment for the partisans, German efforts to stifle the resistance did not succeed. However, this phase of the war in the southeast lies outside of the scope of this study.

The German view of these events which follows was designated as part one of a projected two part historical study. Whether the second part, which would have covered the last two years of the war, was ever written is not known. At any rate, officials of the National Archives in Washington, D.C. have been unable to locate the missing segment. Pre-sumably it does not exist or may never have been written.

The original German text is part of the huge Nuremberg Trial collec-tion of captured German documents amassed as evidence against the Nazi leaders. Thereafter, it gathered dust for three decades in the Na-tional Archives. When I first encountered it in the Archives, it seemed to be merely an interesting account of the war as seen from the German side. Later—in fact, almost a decade later—as I became more deeply immersed in the research literature on the guerrilla war inside the truncated Yugoslav state, the possibility of publishing it in its entirety first occurred to me. An English translation made for the Nuremberg trials contained so many archaisms, gauche constructions, oxymoronisms and howlers of all sorts as to be unusable. The present translation is one which, it is hoped, will be more readable.

The problem of whether to preserve the original language of the document as much as possible at the risk of trying the patience of the reader with all the tedious minutiae of a military historical study was a difficult one. The temptation to delete material and dress up the precise and stilted German military prose into more readable and livelier descriptive language had to be constantly resisted. Apart from some repetitious passages and others which wandered from the point or failed to make one, very little has been excised from the original document.

I would like to acknowledge the assistance offered me by John Taylor of the Old Military Records Division of the National Archives, whose patience in explaining the intricacies of the Nuremberg trial records was of inestimable value. Also, Mr. Robert Wolfe of the German World War II files was equally helpful.

Whenever possible the Serbo-Croatian orthography was used, but occasionally the German or Italian usage (*e.g.*, Laibach, Abbazia) was adhered to as in the original manuscript. The manuscript contained references to many towns and remote villages which the writer has done his best to transcribe in the correct form.

This study was made possible by a grant from the American Philosophical Society.

I

THE POLITICAL AND MILITARY SITUATION IN THE SOUTHEASTERN AREA AFTER THE END OF THE BALKAN CAMPAIGN

1. Regulation of the Chain of Command

When the victorious campaign in the Balkans was concluded by the bold conquest of the island of Crete, and the armed conflict with Russia was already imminent, the Fuehrer and Supreme Commander of the Wehrmacht promoted the Commander in Chief of the 12th Army, Field Marshal List, on June 9, 1941 to the position of Wehrmacht Commander Southeast in order to create a clear and unified chain of command on the Southeastern flank of the Reich.[1]

The Wehrmacht Commander was directly subordinated to the Fuehrer and the OKW. He was the supreme representative of the Wehrmacht in the Balkans and exercized executive powers in the territory occupied exclusively by German troops in the southeastern area with all the powers of a territorial commander in Serbia and Greece. To him were directly subordinated: the *Commander in Serbia* (von Schroeder, General of Anti-Aircraft Artillery), *Commander of the Saloniki-Aegean area* (Major Gen. von Krenski), *Commander in South Greece* (General of the Air Force Felmy), and also for all security and transport questions *Admiral Aegean* and General of the German Army with His Bulgarian Majesty's Supreme Command (Brigadier General Voelkers). The German General in Zagreb, Brigadier General von Glaise Horstenau, was directed to work in cooperation with the Wehrmacht Commander Southeast.

The manifold tasks of the Wehrmacht Commander Southeast extended over all military questions concerning the Wehrmacht, which arose out of the occupation, security and defense of the occupied Southeast area, and the supply, signal and transport organizations on land, sea and in the air. The direction of the air war offensive in the Eastern Mediterranean, which was the concern of the C-in-C of the Air Force and Flight Corps and the operational direction of the war at sea, which remained in the jurisdiction of the C-in-C of the Navy and Admiral Southeast, were excluded from the unified command of the Wehrmacht Commander Southeast.

AOK 12, from which the staff of the Wehrmacht Commander Southeast was formed with allocations from Luftgaukommando Southeast and Admiral Aegean, remained in existence. On May 10 Brigadier General Foertsch took over the tasks of the Chief of the General Staff of the Wehrmacht Commander Southeast and AOK 12 in place of Brigadier General von Greiffenberg who was called away to the East.

2. Drafting of Forces to the Eastern Front

The forces which remained to AOK 12 after the speedy conclusion of the Balkan campaign in the Southeast area were small. Immediately after the capture of Belgrade on April 13, the Panzer-Group of General von Kleist (Headquarters XIV Corps, 11th Panzer Division, 294 Infantry Division, the 4th Mountain Division, Headquarters XXXXI Corps, SS Division "Reich", Infantry Regiment "Grossdeutschland" were separated from the units of the 12th army. In addition, during the operations in Greece, the 9th Panzer Division was held up and withdrawn from the front. In the course of May and June the 2nd, 5th and 16th Panzer Divisions, the 60th Motorized Infantry Division, the Headquarters of XXX, XXXX and L Corps, the 72nd, 73rd, 76th, 198th and 46th Infantry Divisions and the Bodyguard Regiment "Adolf Hitler" also had to be withdrawn for quick rehabilitation at home or immediate allocation to the Eastern Front.

All the fighting forces of the 2nd Army were withdrawn too rapidly after the conclusion of the campaign against Serbia. After the end of the Balkan campaign, AOK 12 had ats its disposal in Greece, only the Headquarters XVIII Corps of General of the Infantry Boehme, the 5th Mountain Division on Crete, the 6th Mountain Division in Attica, and the 164th Infantry Division and 125th Infantry Regiments in Saloniki and on the Aegean islands.

New forces added to AOK 1 (*translator's note*: presumably AOK 12 is meant) were the Commander in Serbia, General of Anti-Aircraft Artillery von Schroder, Corps Command for Special Purposes LXV, under General of Artillery Bader, together with its attached occupation troops in Belgrade, in all, four divisions, the 704th, 714th and 717th in Serbia and the 718th in Croatia. In addition the 713rd Infantry Division joined the 12th Army as replacement for the 5th Mountain Division in Crete.

Pirot and the Macedonian part of the former Yugoslavia, Skoplje, Bitolj, Prilep, and Štip as far as the old Serbo-Greek frontier had been promised to the Bulgars. The Italians had numerous divisions in Albania, the territory north of Lake Ohrida, Kičevo, Tetovo, Prizren and Pristina, as well as in Slovenia. They guarded the Dalmatian coasts and spread later in Croatia, Herzegovina, the southern part of Bosnia and into Slovenia as far as the demarcation line which ran south of Visegrad and Sarajevo and then in a northwesterly direction south of Zagreb.

In the course of the month of June, the 11th Italian Army under General Coloso occupied almost the whole of Greece, the provinces of Attica and Edessa and the Peloponnesus. Only the area of Saloniki, Edessa and Florina, the port of Piraeus, the airfields at Athens, the western half of the island of Crete and the islands of Lemnos, Strathi, Mythilene, Skyros, and Meles still remained in German hands.

The 6th Mountain Division was freed by the Italian occupation of Southern Greece. It left the area of the 12th army in August. As a result of the release of forces made necessary by the Russian campaign. AOK 12 had in the entire Southeast area no full field divisions with the exception of the 5th Mountain Division on Crete, the 164th Infantry Division and the 125th Infantry Regiment in the Saloniki area and on the Aegean islands.

At the end of December 1941, the 5th Mountain Division was also withdrawn from Crete and transferred the the Southeast area. It was replaced by the Fortress Division Crete to be formed from the 164th Infantry Division (without Infantry Regiment 440 which remained as an occupation force on the island) the 713th Infantry Division and Infantry Regiment 125.

The Commanders in Serbia, the Saloniki-Aegean area and Southern Greece exercised executive power in their territories under the supervision of the Wehrmacht Commander Southeast. They were responsible for security and order and for unified defense against attack. The Commander in Serbia was instructed to cooperate directly with the "Reich Plenipotentiary for Economic Affairs". (Exploitation of the country within the meaning of the Four-Year Plan). He had to look after the military administration within his sphere of command. For this, the administrative sub-area and district headquarters, four regional defense battalions and the secret field police were subordinated to him. State Counsellor Dr. Turner was Chief of the Military Administration; Ambassador Dr. Benzler was assigned to the Commander in Serbia as representative of the Foreign Office. The Civil Administration in Serbia was exercised by the "Provisional Serbian Government" with the Serbian authorities in political, economic and cultural spheres under the direction of the Commander in Serbia, the Reich Plenipotentiary for Economic Affairs, NFSK Gruppenfuehrer Neuhausen and later also of the Senior SS and Police Chief, Major-General of the Waffen-SS Meyssner.

Low fighting strength of the Divisions of the 15th Wave

In the event of unrest and uprisings Corps Command for Special Purpose LXV had at its disposal in Old Serbia three divisions, the 704th, the 714th and the 717th. The battalion, section, company and battery leaders had taken part in the First World War, the platoon leaders were 27-37 years old. Only a small number of non-commissioned officers with long service were available. The men were born between 1907 and 1913. The divisions entered Old Serbia as occupation troops under friendly conditions. Their battle training left a lot to be desired. Particularly harmful was the exaggerated setting up of guards everywhere. The unavailable regional defense battalions were insufficient by far to master the numerous security tasks. What did not have to be guarded in Old Serbia: railway lines, bridges, buildings of artistic value, industrial installations, mines, objects of military importance, booty dumps, Air Force ground stations, shipping on the Danube had to be guarded and many other things besides.

The material equipment of these divisions was in no way sufficient. They lacked heavy weapons, motor vehicles, light motor cycles and tires. As the separate battalions of the divisions were stationed in some cases 120 km. apart from each other, this lack of mobility gained all the more importance due to the great distances and bad travel conditions.[2]

In order to relieve the troops of extensive guard duty and to be able to train them better, Corps Command LXV proposed the bringing up of further regional defense battalions as reinforcement. OKH however was unable to satisfy these justified demands because of the necessary employment of all available regional defense battalions in the extensive area of the Russian theatre of war.

In order to equip the divisions with heavy weapons for combatting any unrest, and to make them more mobile, an infantry howitzer platoon and a panzer platoon (reconnaissance section) had to be set up with each regiment, and, with each division, a mountain artillery battery with access to stocks of booty and captured vehicles.[3] But available signals material, in particular radio equipment were completely insufficient. Therefore a mixed signals company had to be set up for each division and telephone platoons and radio troops changed into telephone companies and radio companies respectively.

3. Conditions in Serbia and Croatia

After the unprecedented collapse in Yugoslavia at the end of June, the idea of a Greater Serbia arose in Old Serbia on the right bank of the Drina. During the swift campaign in Serbia, the country could not be entirely pacified by our troops and cleared of the remnants of the Yugoslav Army. A large number of officers and soldiers (about 300,000) of the former Yugoslav Army were not captured. An abundance of weapons, ammunition and war equipment remained in the country.

Shortly after the outbreak of the German-Russian war in the days when the last big troop transports were leaving the Balkans for the east, the first signs of an insurgent movement flared up in Serbia. Placards and leaflets summoned people all over the country to plunder, sabotage and riot. In Belgrade the cable of the propaganda company's radio transmitter was cut and an attempt to blow up the transmitter with explosives was prevented. Railway lines were torn up, telephone communications were broken, Serbian gendarmerie stations were attacked and German Wehrmacht vehicles were fired on. Kindled by Russian and English propaganda, which easily penetrated the disturbed country, and by communist, and probably also Serbian national agitation, local unrest flared up everywhere. In Belgrade and other places those acts of sabotage were followed immediately by interrogations, arrests and the shooting of Communists and Jews. Clemency could not be shown under the existing conditions.

At the beginning of July armed bands appeared for the first time in the district of Arandjelevac northwest of Topola. It was striking that generals of the former Yugoslav army joined these gangs. About this time riots were reported west of the Drina, in Herzegovina east of Nevesinje in the area held by the Italians.

Disturbing elements also developed in the newly emerging Croatian state. With the collapse of Yugoslavia, Croatia had been recognized as an independent state by the Axis Powers and maintained friendly relations with Germany. After the departure of the 2nd army, the country remained occupied by only the most necessary German troops, the 714th Infantry Division which was subordinated to Corps Command LXV, and 4 regional defense battalions. This weak occupation force was to remain in Croatia however only until the young state established itself, constructed its Wehrmacht, and unrest had subsided. It was of advantage to preserve law and order there because of the important interests related to the war economy which the Reich had in Croatia.

However unrest spread over the entire country. It soon became apparent that in this old storm-center of Europe on both sides of the Drina it was not a question of isolated, local robber bands, but of an incipient insurgent movement of communist and Serbian nationalist forces. The almost inaccessible mountain country facilitated the clandestine organization of the insurgent movement in that it provided many hiding places for the insurgent bands.

II

THE BEGINNING OF THE INSURGENT MOVEMENT
SERBIA AND CROATIA

JULY TO AUGUST 1941

1. Sabotage and Surprise Attacks

July 1941

The Communist acts of sabotage which began shortly after the outbreak of the German-Russian war persisted throughout the whole month of July. Serbian police and gendarmerie patrols were attacked by bandits, gendarmerie stations were attacked and community offices pillaged. In the countryside clashes occurred between the Serbian gendarmerie and the bands. The Serbian police and gendarmerie were practically powerless against these bands which appeared in ever increasing numbers and were often supported by the population. In addition available German security forces, field police and local guards were no longer sufficient for guarding the military installations, railway lines and art works. Therefore reinforcements from the widely scattered forces billeted in Serbia had to be transported to the endangered areas. Acts of sabotage occurred against German Wehrmacht property: saboteurs burned captured aircraft at Jagodina airfield and in Belgrade a large part of a vehicle park was destroyed by fire. As reprisal for such attacks upon German police patrols, numerous Communists and Jews were shot or executed.

Conditions were not much better in Croatia. There and in Serbia, important railway lines had been repeatedly interrupted by acts of sabotage, e.g., the lines connecting Banja Luka-Prijedor-Bos.Novi, Zagreb-Split, Zagreb-Belgrade and others. South of the Serbian capital railway viaducts were blown up and for the first time a leave train from the front was fired on between Lapovo and Palanka. Thereafter leave trains from the front were guarded by escort detachments as well as thoroughfares and railraods to ensure the safety of traffic. Even in northern Banat, in the area of Petrovgrad-Malenci-Kumane, communist bands were rife, destroying large stores of wheat. Stronger forces, two battalions of Infantry Regiment 721 of the 704th Infantry Division, were brought up against these robber bands at the end of July.

Since the first flare-up of this insurgent movement, as previously mentioned, units of the 704th, 714th, 717th, and 718th Infantry divisions had been brought up to combat the communist bands, as the police and gendarmerie were no longer sufficient to uphold the peace and security of the country. But in spite of numerous, small engagements the troops were unable to quell the insurgents. They had neither the requisite mobility, training, nor the psychological preparation. Everywhere terror bands appeared and carried on determined, small scale struggles, making full use of treachery, cunning and the diversity of the country—dense maize fields in the plains and mountain country covered with underbrush. These insurgents could not be captured with individual small units whose mobility was impaired by lack of vehicles, because the former could always quickly withdraw to inaccessible hiding places in the mountain country. The insurgents could only be fought successfully by completely oriented, fully mobile units, well trained in guerrilla warfare.

2. The First Directives for the Combatting of Bands

Therefore, about the middle of July, Corps Command LXV found itself charged with the task of informing the subordinate divisions that the enemy's position was not always clear to the troops. Rumors were often false or exaggerated. Also it was inadvisable to throw in weak units against the insurgents when the situation was unclarified. The guiding principle in combatting the bands should be to approach the given task with as strong a force as possible, with reinforced battalions, regiments and under certain conditions even with whole divisions, and also, if at all possible with artillery. It was important to cut off the centers of unrest before the attack, in order to prevent the insurgents from escaping. (Those of Slatina [District of Bor] and southwest of Čačak).[1]

> Field Marshal List had already given directives for the combatting of bands in his conferences on July 21 in Niš with the Commanding General of Corps Command LXV, General of Artillery Bader and the Commander of the 717th Infantry Division, Brigadier General Hoffmann, and on July 22 and 23 in Belgrade with the Commander of the 714th Infantry Division, Brigadier General Stahl, the 704th Infantry Division, Brigadier General Borofsky and the 718th Infantry Division, Brigadier General Fortner. On August 13, with the return of the Commander in Chief from Vienna, the problems of the insurgent movement were also discussed with Commander in Serbia, General of the Air Force Dankelmann, in the special train in Belgrade.

At the beginning of July 7th as the increasing acts of sabotage in Serbia and in the parts of Croatia occupied by German troops left little doubt of a general uprising, the Wehrmacht Commander Southeast requested the OKW to set up an air force training school in the Serbian area, since operational air units were not yet available for the swift suppression of unrest.

3. Beginning of the Combatting of Bands According to Plan
August 1941

At the beginning of August the situation in Serbia was still strained, and troops of the 704th, 714th, 717th and 718th Infantry Divisions had been employed on occasion against the bands. Acts of sabotage and attacks apparently carried out according to plan, were directed more and more against the Wehrmacht. The terror perpetrated by the Communist and Serbian nationalist bands was also directed against the population which suffered terribly. Violent disruption of the country's political and economic life had not yet occurred, however, and the Commander in Serbia described the populace's cooperation with the Administrative Serbian Government and the Serbian police as good. In general the majority of the Serbian population conducted itself loyally towards the German occupying force. The alleged imminent transfer of the Banat to Hungary and of Semlin to Croatia added greatly to the disturbance among the Serbs and also among the Germans, Bulgars and Hungarians living there. In addition the terrible deprivation of the fugitives which resulted from the mass expulsions of Serbs from Croatia, provided good ground for insidious Communist agitation and for the furthering of the Communist movement. With a further aggravation of the situation, the terrorist bands could move to a greater armed uprising.

In Croatia widespread unrest flared up, caused by armed bands previously active only in the area southwest of Banja Luka. Excesses by the Ustasha had certainly led to this unrest. The insurgents were fought by the fledgling Croatian Wehrmacht and the expansion of the Communist movement from Serbia to Croatia seemed possible. Previously only one attack on German Wehrmacht installations had been reported. In the event that German Wehrmacht interests were endangered, strong intervention by the 178th Infantry Division in close cooperation with the German General in Zagreb was provided for. On August 13 the German General in Zagreb was authorized by an order from the Wehrmacht Commander Southeast to request the employment of troops of the 718th Infantry Division on his own responsibility in urgent cases.

Since the beginning of the Russian campaign increased communist propaganda took place in the southern part of Serbia. The acts of sabotage carried out there, particularly against the railways, were probably of Communist origin.

In agreement with the suggestions made by the Wehrmacht Commander Southeast, C-in-C Air Force had training units of the Luftwaffe transferred to Zagreb and Semlin, in order to conduct straffing operations if necessary. In the first part of August at the suggestion of the Wehrmacht Commander Southeast a bomber unit was formed in Zagreb from these training units and committed to combat the insurgents. But on the 4th of August, Luftwaffe Operations Staff ordered the disbanding of this bomber unit and its relocation to home bases due to a lack of suitable attack targets. However, they remained on the alert in the event of larger bands appearing in the disturbed areas, which occupied villages and could be attacked effectively from the air. Flight Corps X was also asked by Wehrmacht Commander Southeast to make available aircraft to combat the insurgents, but refused this request with the approval of C-in-C Luftwaffe on the grounds that Flight Corps X was unable to give up forces to combat the insurgents without endangering the execution of its assigned tasks in the Mediterranean and North Africa. In addition the combatting of insurgents in the Balkans by the Luftwaffe would be unsuccessful owing to unsuitable targets.

Wehrmacht Commander Southeast had repeatedly requested the reinforcement of the occupation troops in Serbia by regional defense battalions. But on 7 August OKW announced that the handing over of the battalions was impossible owing to the tasks in the East which for the time being were more urgent. Two days later OKH also refused to release to Belgrade the regional defense battalions intended for Croatia, as these battalions could be made available only temporarily. As a substitute, OKH had in view the reinforcement of Regional Defense Battalion 562 in Belgrade by the setting up of two new companies.

On August 10th, the Wehrmacht Commander Southeast decided to subordinate temporarily to Corps Command LXV the anti-tank battalion of the 164th Infantry Division in addition to a number of captured tanks already handed over, in order to partially relieve the lack of mobility of the unit.

Directives for the combatting of bands.

The next day, on August 11th the Commander in Serbia charged the LXV Corps Command with the task of "immediately carrying out offensive warfare against the Communist bands." Additionally, he indicated that apart from the directives already under the LXV Corps Command for the combatting of insurgents, the psychological and educational preparation of the troops was absolutely necessary in order to permit the successful execution of this offensive war. The divisions under the LXV Corps Command had entered Serbia under peaceful conditions and had carried on their training only as occupation troops. "Now under completely altered conditions, I know of no occupation unit in Serbia, except one, trained to be a fighting unit. Quick use of weapons, sudden changes and the combing of farms, villages, woods and maize fields are necessary. That is training in guerrilla warfare."

In every battalion a pursuit detachment of 30-50 men was to be set up immediately, preferably from volunteers, under trusted, brave, and aggressive leaders. These detachments were to be equipped with trucks, light and heavy machine guns, submachine guns, hand grenades, adequate ammunition, fuel and supplies. Armored reconnaissance, cars, motorcycles, signal equipment and radios, were to be allocated to these pursuit detachments according to their needs. They would also be supplemented by Serbian gendarmerie and auxiliary forces as well as interpreters.

Meanwhile events in Serbia caused the Chief of the General Staff of the Wehrmacht Commander Southeast to summon a meeting (12 August) at Defissia, with the German General in Zagreb, Brigadier General von Glaise Horstenau and the Chief of the General Staff of the Commander in Serbia, Lt. Colonel Gravenhorst, for a report on the situation in Serbia and Croatia and to draw up directives for combatting the insurgents.

Intensification of the situation.

Towards the end of August the situation in Serbia had once again become tense. Acts of terror and sabotage on the part of the bandits, especially on railways and bridges, surprise attacks on German soldiers, gendarmerie quarters and salvage dumps were being reported daily in increasing numbers.

A localised increase in unrest occurred. For the moment the main insurgent areas were situated in Old Serbia (except the Banat and the Albanian enclave near Mitrovica), on the Serbian-Croatian border, and in the area of Valjevo-Ljubovije-Drina. Whether the Četniks were also supporting the Communists, was still not known. Nevertheless it was obvious that many Četniks at least behaved in a passive manner as far as the insurgents were concerned. Indeed the Commander in Serbia indicated at this time that collaboration with the newly appointed Serbian Government under Nedić was good. In contrast to this, the Wehrmacht Commander Southeast believed that the Serbian Government was scarcely willing or capable of taking any energetic action against the insurgents. Up until now a pacification of the country by the Nedić government had not taken place.

In their fight against the insurgents the German troops could list local successes, for example, on the Serbian-Croatian border. In the last days of August, a rather large operation by a reinforced pursuit detachment, supported by aircraft, was underway near Šabac. At the end of the month the 164th Infantry Division had to give up the III Battalion of the 433rd Infantry Regiment as reinforcement for the LXV Corps Command in Belgrade.

In Croatia the unrest which broke out here and there could be put down until now by the German and Croatian troops. However, bands which had been driven out of Serbia were now active in Croatia. A new center of unrest near Bos. Kostajnica was mopped up by Croatian troops, with the help of German troops and aircraft.

III

THE SUPPRESSION OF THE REVOLT IN SERBIA

SEPTEMBER TO DECEMBER 1941

1. The outbreak of a systematic revolt in Serbia

Between the end of August and the beginning of September a further intensification of the situation in Serbia took place. Surprise attacks on German soldiers, Wehrmacht vehicles, and Serbian gendarmerie posts again increased. Wehrmacht freight and passenger trains were fired on, railroad installations were destroyed, bridges blown up, railroad security attacked and freight cars plundered. All these surprise attacks were concentrated mainly on the Belgrade-Užice-Ćuprija-Paraćin-Zajecar line. On August 31 alone, 18 surprise attacks on railroad stations and railway lines were carried out. Daily surprise attacks on railroads and gendarmerie posts, as well as acts of sabotage on long distance telephone lines threatened to break down all communication.

Due to Communist actions a large number of the Serbian coal and metal mines were not working. Where work was still in progress ore shipments were considerably affected by the many railroad breakdowns. In addition to these continually increasing terror and sabotage acts, surprise attacks on Serbian community offices increased. Records of the Serbian civilian administration were burned everywhere and financial offices were robbed, making an orderly administration of the country impossible. Complete anarchy reigned in the country.

In August 242 attempts on the authorities, gendarmerie posts, railroads, long distance telephone wires, mines and industrial undertakings were reported. 22 soldiers were killed and 17 wounded. By September 1st the losses increased considerably.

In the rugged mountains and woods of Serbia, many Serbian nationalist bands, partisans and Četniks were hidden. They received numerous additions from the still quite considerable remnants of the Yugoslav army which had not been destroyed during the lightning advance in April. Thousands of captured Serbian officers and men were set free by our troops. When they were threatened with being taken into captivity again, many of these officers and men fled into the mountains.

In the Balkans, life counts for nothing, one's own life for very little. Insurgent and bandit movements had always been prevalent and most persons carried weapons. After the unparalleled collapse of the Yugoslav state, the insurgent movement which flared up shortly after the outbreak of the German-Russian war was exacerbated by the actions of the surrounding states. From the territory between the Theiss and the Danube which had been turned over to Hungary, more than 37,000 Serbs, about 100,000 from Croatia, and approximately 20,000 from Bulgarian Macedonia crowded into the remaining Serbian territory. Without any belongings and in the most abject condition, many among these hordes of refugees had witnessed the murder of their loved ones. They had nothing more to lose. With their sudden influx into Old Serbia, they could neither be placed or billeted anywhere. Therefore they allied themselves by the thousands to the bands.

After the outbreak of the German-Russian war the insurgent movement in Serbia continued to grow. From the beginning it was supported not only by communist but also by Serbian nationalist and Pan-Slav ideas.

Since the Serbian security forces were not able to maintain order and security in the country, the German Commander in Serbia considered an immediate reinforcement and a further arming of the Serbian police and gendarmerie as essential in order to avoid, wherever possible, the commitment of German troops and to remove a burden from the German security forces. Furthermore only a few troops were available in Serbia and these were neither sufficiently trained nor equipped for band warfare. With these forces alone the revolt could no longer be suppressed. Even with the most unrestricted reprisal measures—up until the end of August a total of approximately 1,000 Communists and Jews had been shot or publicly hanged and the houses of the guilty burned down—it was not possible to restrain the continual growth of the armed revolt. Even with the help of the provisional government, which was generally regarded as the bailiff of the occupation power, and which had little authority among the people, it was not possible to eradicate the danger. Therefore the Chief of Staff of the Commander in Serbia, General Staff Colonel Kewisch, and the German political representatives in Belgrade (Consul Neuhausen and Ambassador Benzler) believed that they would find a solution by trying to win the cooperation of larger circles of the Serbian population, and by separating from the Communist bands the Četnik bands, whose leader, Pećanac apparently enjoyed great support and respect among the Serbian people, and was feted almost as a national hero.

Reformation of the Serbian Government

At the end of August an attempt was made to form a new Serbian government which would find support among the people. It was necessary to put at the head of the government a man who not only enjoyed the respect and trust of the population which still behaved in a peaceful manner, but also that of the former Serbian officers who had fled to the bands. This requirement was satisfied in the person of the former Yugoslav general Nedić, known to have been an opponent of Minister President Simović who had fled. In addition, during his period of office as Minister of War, he had worked for the pact with Germany and was regarded as a strong man and as an enemy of communism. In his government there were three supporters of the Ljotić party, from whom a lot was expected. Even before the creation of the new government, Nedić gained some support from a large number of the Četnik bands under the leadership of Vojvoda Pećanac which declared themselves ready not only to stand aloof from communism, but also to take part in the fight against the communist bands.[1]

The Nedić government was given permission by the Commander in Serbia to reinforce the Serbian gendarmerie up to a strength of 5,000. Furthermore, it was allowed to create an "Auxiliary Fighting Force" from the local population, in limited numbers and under German supervision. For industrial plants a factory guard with 250 Volksdeutsch as cadre was created.

The Wehrmacht Commander Southeast was somewhat surprised about the reorganization of the government since he had not been informed about it but was presented with a fait accompli. Retroactive permission was given despite some reservations. Later it became apparent that the decision to make use of the Četniks in the fight against the alleged communist bands was a danger in itself, and moreover the arming of the Serbian gendarmerie, which had shown itself neither capable nor willing to foght against the insurgents, was a doubtful measure.

The Chief of the General Staff of the 12th Army, Generalmajor Foertsch, who on September 1st delivered to the Commander in Serbia and to the LXV Corps Command the combat directives of Field Marshal List—immediate counter attacks, few prisoners, effective defense—reported on the creation of the government: "My impression is that this is an undertaking whose success must be awaited. Downright violence still remains as the last resort." Equally, the Wehrmacht Commander Southeast did not share the great hopes placed in the Nedić government by the Commander in Serbia.

Difficult Situation of the German Occupation Forces

In the meantime violent guerrilla warfare had flared up between our fighter detachments and the bands. In the course of these conflicts some successes were achieved: during an operation south of Belgrade 26 Communists and their leader were killed. Near Zlot, northwest of Zaječar, a German pursuit detachment freed some Serbian gendarmerie and German soldiers captured by the bandits. Stukas were also committed against rather large bands which threatened the copper mines at Bor. Bands were also driven from Topola, west of Kruševac, from Svrlig, northwest of Niš and near Paraćin by our pursuit detachments.

In the area between the Sava and the Drina, well-armed and well-led bands were active. Here a really threatening insurgent movement flared up. Six companies were committed against snipers in the area of Loznica-Čačak-Bogatić. In the beginning of September our troops suffered serious setbacks. One company, which was surrounded by insurgents near Koviljače, southwest of Loznica, had to be evacuated by airlift. Moreover the garrison of the antimony works at Krupanje, consisting of two companies was surrounded by numerous bands and completely cut off. In spite of the committment of several companies from Valjevo and from the west across the Drina and the additional support of Stukas, the beleaguered companies could not be freed from their encirclement in time. The advance of our troops in this mountain range, full of gorges, was greatly hindered by road blocks and the swollen state of the river. The two German companies encircled in the antimony works at Krupanj were destroyed by the bandits. Our losses of 9 dead, 30 wounded and 175 missing were deplorable.

Undoubtedly the three divisions of the 15th wave in Serbia, and the reinforcements which were sent to Belgrade were inadequate to protect all the important strong points. Only a concentration of forces could remove the danger of post after post being destroyed by the insurgents, and of the widely dispersed garrisons being destroyed one after another.

Reinforcements for Serbia

As soon as Field Marshal List was cognizant of these setbacks, he instructed the Commander in Serbia and the LXV Corps Command on September 4th: "Be ready to use the most rigorous means possible to quash the insurgent movement in the area of Krupanje and Koviljače. For this purpose, all forces which are available anywhere (also artillery) are to be committed under a unified leadership (division commander)."

At the same time, the Corps Headquarters of the XVIII Infantry Corps was instructed to transport the I and II Battalions, 433 Infantry Regiment, 164th Infantry Division, with one Artillery Battalion without delay to the LXV Corps Command in Belgrade, as the situation in Serbia demanded the immediate reinforcement of the forces here. Yet on the 4th, the battle-tested 125th Infantry Regiment was destined for commitment against the insurgents instead of the two battalions of the 433 Infantry Regiment. When an inquiry arrived on September 5 from the OKW as to what measures were being taken to quash the revolt, the Wehrmacht Commander Southeast was able to reply that a Panzer Jaeger Battalion and the III Battalion of the 433 Infantry Regiment of the 164th Infantry Division had been dispatched to the Corps Command a long time ago, and that the transfer of further combat troops from the 125 Infantry Regiment and an artillery battalion was being arranged.

The serious occurrences in Serbia moreover caused Field Marshal List to issue new explicit directives concerning the conduct of the war against the insurgents, to the Commander in Serbia and to the LXV Corps Command.

"Further progress of the insurgent movement does not appear impossible, judging by the situation in Serbia. Increased attacks on soldiers and Wehrmacht installations by strong, well armed, organized and cleverly led bands are proof that the counter measures taken up until now are not sufficient. Therefore the Command in Serbia and the Corps Command must make all preparations in order to prevent any worsening of the situation, and to pacify the country before the beginning of the winter."

"In this matter one had to make allowances for the following points of view: the more tense the situation in Serbia becomes, the more the troops must be concentrated, with regard to the main point of attack, and locally within the insurgent territory, in the area of Šabac-Valjevo-Krupanje-Loznica-Topola-Kragujevac-Užice-Lazarevac   and Bor-Zajecar-Niš-Kruševac. Localities are not to be garrisoned below battalion strength.

"Surprise attacks upon and sudden destruction of the insurgent centers by means of encirclement with superior forces, including artillery, command of the operations by older, experienced officers (division commanders), detailed, fixed operational plans, and prior reconnoitering and reconnaissance are strongly recommended. The fighter detachments which have been committed up until now are obviously not sufficient.

"The present widely dispersed posts and the effort to guard and protect everything at the same time conceals the great danger of dispersion. Of necessity setbacks must follow. Therefore protection must be confined if necessary to such objects, the preservation of which are essential, above all, Belgrade, the capital, the Leskovac-Niš-Velgrade-Zagreb railroad, the bridges over the Danube and the Sava, the Danube breach at the Iron Gate and the copper mines at Bor. Also the use of every available kind of active, vigorous propaganda.

"Increased pressure on the population in whose territory insurgents are permitted in order to force the inhabitants to notify the German authorities of the appearance of bands, or otherwise to cooperate in rendering harmless the centers of unrest.

"Immediate ruthless measures against the insurgents, their accomplices and their dependents. Strict supervision of the Serbian gendarmerie. Increased use of agents to identify the ring-leaders, string-pullers and the centers of revolt. Greater employment of the influence of the government, which is to be drawn into active cooperation. All members of the German Wehrmacht in Serbia were to be instructed continually concerning the situation in Serbia and their behavior when attacked. Initiative and action were demanded of every German soldier." The order closed with the words:

> I demand from the troop leaders of every rank, special activity and initiative, as well as their complete personal commitment to the task set for them, which at the moment consists simply and solely of destroying completely and conclusively the Serbian insurgent movement.

On the same day (September 5) as Field Marshal List published these basic directives for the destruction of the insurgent movement, a new emergency call from Belgrade arrived in his headquarters from the Commander, Serbia: "In case the bringing up of a powerful division, which has been requested many times, is not possible, please effect the transfer of a replacement division into the Serbian area."

In the meantime the situation in Serbia had again become more acute. The attacks of the bands which were apparently led according to plan, and the numerous surprise attacks on traffic lines, industrial plants, as well as the daily acts of sabotage on railroads continued, particularly in the area north of the line Aleksinac-Kruševac-Kraljevo-Užice. Open revolt was also reported in the territory around Bor. Near Šabac and near Lazarevac as well as between Valjevo and Krupanje and in the area west of Užice, strong, well-armed and cleverly led bands had flocked together during the first week of September. The Wehrmacht Commander was perfectly aware that it was not only a case of a communist, but of a general, national Serbian insurgent movement. Therefore Field Marshal List did not acknowledge in any way the view of the Commander in Serbia, that they must reinforce and provide the Serbian gendarmerie with better arms, and even make use of national Serbian Četnik units to combat the "so-called communist" bands in order to quell the revolt, particularly if sufficient forces were lacking.

Reports had already arrived, that the Serbian gendarmerie had allowed itself to be disarmed by the insurgents without offering any resistance, and that Serbian gendarmes suspected of favoring the insurgents had been arrested by our combat detachments. Gendarmes appeared to have even taken part in acts of sabotage on the Paraćin-Zaječar line.

Under these conditions, the Wehrmacht Commander Southeast was doubtful from the beginning of the success of the new Serbian Government of General Nedić, which was formed in Belgrade at the end of August, without his knowledge and without his consent having been obtained beforehand. Not until September 3 did the Commander Serbia report fully concerning the motives which had led to the reformation of the government.

On September 8 a letter arrived from Belgrade from the Chief of the General Staff to the Ia of the 12th Army. General Foertsch, on August 31, on the occasion of a journey to Berlin, brought to the Commander Serbia and to the LXV Corps Command the propaganda and battle directives of Field Marshal List: immediate counter attacks, not too many prisoners, effective defense. In this letter he described the reformation of the government as "an attempt, the success of which has to be awaited." "Outright violence," he stated, "still remains as the last resort." At the same time he declared: "The government has received permission from the Commander in Serbia to reinforce the Gendarmerie up to 5,000 men. In addition it may form an "auxiliary fighting force" from local inhabitants. An attempt should be made to incorporate the Četniks. Limited numbers, lists under supervision and the closest liaison without troops are to be secured. (No operations of their own without permission, participation in unit operations)."

Along these lines the Chief of the General Staff, Field Marshal List reported to the OKW on September 8 regarding the new Serbian government:

"The reformation of the Serbian government, with the intention of drawing Serbian national circles into an active cooperation is a venture whose success must await a further increase in the insurgent movement.

"The scale of the struggles, the fact that two insurgents are for the most part, well-armed, and obviously also skillfully directed, leads to the conclusion that the Serbian national movement—perhaps also the Četniks—are working somehow hand in hand with the so-called Communists. In addition, wherever the Serbian gendarmerie was not working directly with German units, it has shown itself to be unreliable, or has behaved in a purely passive manner.

"The task of the German occupation forces still remains that of suppressing the insurgent movement with all available means and by exhausting all possibilities. Concerning this the Commander in Serbia too has no doubts. In my order of September 5th I pointed this out to him once more, as well as the measures which appear necessary to this end. At the same time I conveyed to him the interpretation of the insurgent movement which I have just described, and suggested to him that the greatest care be taken with regard to the further arming of the Serbian police and purportedly reliable Serbs.

"I am also of the opinion that the four divisions of the 15th Wave, which are subordinate to the LXV Corps Command, three of them in the Serbian area, and one in the Croatian area, are not sufficient as regards numbers, actual composition armament, equipment and training to quickly destroy the insurgent movement once and for all. I have therefore repeatedly requested more strong, mobile units for Serbia, which, however, have not been furnished. With this means at my disposal I have tried to reach a compromise so that the Panzer Jaeger Battalion and the III Battalion of the 433 Infantry Regiment and the 164 Infantry Division, have been subordinated to the LXV Corps Command, and the whole of the 125 Infantry Regiment with one artillery battalion has been transported to Serbia.

"These reinforcements however will not suffice. Therefore I again propose the transport of at least one powerful division to Serbia, and in case this is not possible, at least the quick transfer of one replacement division. Independent of all this, the rapid transport of more tanks, armored patrol cars and armored trains from captured Russian material cannot be postponed any longer. The Renault tanks which have been assigned up until now, have proved for the most part to be unusable or in need of repair."[2]

As already mentioned, the Nedic government was formed without the prior consent of the Wehrmacht Commander Southeast having been obtained. Field Marshal List first learned that the concession of reinforcing and arming the gendarmerie had been made to this government, through a September 4 notice in the field newspaper "Wacht im Suedosten" (Watch in the Southeast), then through a telephone report of the Commander Serbia and a radio message on September 6. Two days later on September 8 a radio message of the OKW stated:

"According to a report of the German Information Bureau, Belgrade office, September 6, General Nedic is said to have issued a proclamation to the Serbian people, in which he resolved to enforce respect for the existing laws in Serbia, if necessary by military means. The proclamation is said to have decreed newly created armed formations of the Serbian army within the framework of a military call-up. The Fuehrer demands a report by return post and requests unequivocal confirmation that the creation of any formations whatsoever of the Serbian army will under no circumstances be allowed. Only a limited reinforcement of the Gendarmerie, but not with heavy weapons, will be considered."

On September 9th the Wehrmacht Commander Southeast transmitted to the OKW the explanation submitted by the Commander Serbia: "Only limited reinforcement of the Gendarmerie and the Police, without heavy weapons [is] granted to the Serbian government in cooperation with the Commander Serbia. All other news is a fabrication." The next day, on September 10 Field Marshal List informed the Commander Serbia, that he had first learned from a newspaper announcement that certain concessions of a basic nature had been made to the new Serbian government. "Since, by the Fuehrer directive No. 31 of June 9th I was expressly charged with the supervision of the administration exercised by the Commanders in territories occupied by German troops, I must attach great importance to being informed in advance of such significant understandings. I have already referred both orally and in writing to the necessity of exercizing the greatest care in the reinforcing and the further arming of the Serbian gendarmerie. This caution is also necessary in the arming of all other Serbs (factory guards, etc.). The expression, "Armed Power" (Bewaffnete Macht) which appeared in the newspaper notice and in the radio speech of the Serbian Minister President, has as is to be expected, given rise to repeated inquiries from the highest authorities. It must disappear. The word "Militia" (Miliz) is also out of place because it suggests armed power. The setting up of such a Serbian Militia may not be considered under any circumstances. I can only give my consent to a further arming (under no circumstance with heavy arms) of the Gendarmerie, when it is certain that the Serbian Gendarmerie will behave in a loyal and reliable manner and has proved itself in action. Moreover I again request that care be taken that in the future that all important affairs and reports are channelled through the Wehrmacht Commander Southeast and not directly conveyed to the highest authorities."[3]

Suggestions of Field Marshal List to the OKW

On September 11 Field Marshal List informed Major General Foertsch, who after his talks in Belgrade had left for Berlin, by teletype of the present situation in Serbia:

"Armed revolt of organized, cleverly led and well armed bands (not only Communists). Centers of the revolt: Drina-Sava triangle (district of Loznica-Krupanje), area of Ub-Lazarevac and the district of Bor. Increasing sabotage according to plan on railroads and long distance communications. Serbian gendarmerie repeatedly unreliable. A further increase of the insurgent movement is to be expected. Banat, Albanian territory and Belgrade still quiet. Pursuit detachments no longer sufficient. Setbacks have already occurred even with stronger units. Our own losses in the last 10 days, approximately 400, including missing and deserters. 125 Infantry Regiment and one artillery battalion on the way to Serbia. These reinforcements are not sufficient, therefore urgent and speedy transport of further powerful and mobile troops as well as tanks and armoured trains available for employment from captured Russian material proposed. Replacement division requested and prospects held out for same."

Major General Foertsch was commissioned to inform the members of the Wehrmacht High Command concerning the situation in Serbia. In so doing he had to point out the "limited capacity of the divisions of the 15th Wave for commitment, of their insufficient composition as regards men and material, their inadequate training and leadership."

The OKW was again requested to quickly transport to Serbia, a powerful front line unit, at least a division—apart from the Panzer forces already proposed, since otherwise further unacceptable setbacks would not be avoided. Field Marshal List laid particular emphasis on the intolerable chain of command: "In Serbia authority is based on peace time and not on war conditions. The Military Commander is a territorial and at the same time supreme troop commander. The position should be filled by an older, well schooled general who has had front line experience. The composition of the staff must also satisfy this requirement as well as the interests of the Four Year Plan. The condition for the realization of these [interests] is security and order in the country."

"The breakdown in connection with the reformation of the government," said Field Marshal List at the end of his teletype message to Major General Foertsch, "could only happen because, on the basis of former directives from above and customs prior to the establishment of the Wehrmacht Commander Southeast, the Military Commander Serbia believed he could act independently. I hope I have been successful in getting rid of this concept. A brake has been applied to [Serbian] reinforcements, and they will be supervised; in no case will there be heavy weapons. The setting up of Self-Defense units (Selbstschutz), erroneously designated Militia, has been deterred for the present."[4]

Field Marshal List transmitted the same suggestions, also in a teltype message (September 12) to the OKW and the OKH:

"Threatening development of the overall situation in Serbia demands energetic measures. Even the new Serbian government does not come up to expectations, according to reports of the Commander in Serbia. Gendarmerie unreliable on an increasing scale. Association between the insurgents—in my opinion not aptly described as Communists by the Commander in Serbia—with the Četniks, had been confirmed. The first requisite is a rigid, uniform leadership of the offensive operations which are necessary for the restoration of unconditional authority. Moreover it is essential that the overall executive power, including command over the troops which will be committed, should be united in one person, i.e., a supreme troop commander. The present command regulations are based on peacetime conditions and are untenable under the present turbulent combat conditions. General of Infantry Boehme may be considered as especially suitable for this position, as he has an excellent understanding of conditions in the Balkans. He and his staff could be made available for this task.

"Even after transfer of the reinforced 125th Infantry regiment, the German forces are in no way sufficient for carrying out the necessary operations in Serbia. The divisions of the 15th Wave, both as regards personnel and material composition, as well as leadership, are unsuitable, in light of previous experience, for the destruction of this expanding revolt. Mobile supply installations for larger sized operations are also lacking.

"I am therefore forced, despite my evaluation of the overall situations, to propose the urgent transport of at least one powerful frontline division with tank support."[5]

Situation in Belgrade

Captain (cavalry) Campe, the special-missions staff officer, who had delivered to Belgrade the September 5 order for the suppression of the Serbian insurgent movement, reported (September 9) the following on the situation in Belgrade:

"There is a major difference of opinion between the Commander in Serbia General der Flieger Dankelmann and the Commanding General of the LXV Corps Command General Bader with respect to the new Serbian government and the employment of Serbian forces in the battle against the Communists. The Commander in Serbia has utmost confidence in the Nedić government as well as in the Četnik units which are under the direction of Colonel Pećanac. Through contacts Colonel Pećanac has offered to fight the Communists with his units. Subsequent negotiations between the Commander in Serbia, the new Serbian government and the Četniks led to an agreement whereby the Commander recognized the Četniks and gave them the right to recruit openly, and carry arms. In return the Četniks have pledged themselves to fight against the Communists.

"The government was given the right to strengthen its armed forces. By recruiting officers and non-commissioned officers of the old Serbian army the strength of the Gendarmerie—hitherto 2 to 3,000 men—has been increased to 5,000 men. In addition an auxiliary police force has been set up and a type of militia consisting of local inhabitants has been organized in the various localities. For this purpose the government has thus far been provided with 15,000 rifles and a fairly large number of machine guns by the Commander (Serbia). Consequently the Četniks are appearing openly and recruiting in the villages. However, it is uncertain whether the Pećanac Četniks despite the agreements, are not supporting the ever increasing bandit activity. Hence the [German] forces complain of an intolerable confusion and uncertainty, for they are expected to resist the Communist bands, but are not permitted to do anything to the Četniks although in many instances there is no distinction between Communists and Četniks.

"General Bader and Colonel Kewisch (Chief of General Staff of LXV Corps Command) do not trust the Četniks. Orders have already been found which prove that the Četniks and Communists have been collaborating. At LXV Corps Command there is the belief that the decision of the Commander in Serbia to use the Serbian government and the Četniks in the fight against the communist bands might lead to two great dangers. The Četniks might soon join forces with the

Communists and against the German occupation troops. Secondly the Serbian government and the Četniks might restore peace in the land and at the same time be obliged to contend with the prospect of a dangerous revolt without being in a position to counteract it in due time. For the government and the Četniks will claim credit for having restored peace in the land whereas the Germans were not in a position to do so."

In concluding this letter Captain Campe reported that "something must be done as soon as possible to avoid being faced with new surprises in Serbia which might have serious course import." Lt. Colonel Gravenhorst, Chief of Staff in Serbia informed him that the existing difficulties could not be obviated with the forces presently available. If they did not use Serbian support, then there was only one alternative: to permit the neighboring nationalities to enter Serbia and to let them restore peace by destroying the seditious elements in the populace. Such a decision, which of course could only be made in Berlin, would be welcomed by the Hungarians, Croats, Albanians and Bulgarians. But the result would be that Serbia would be withdrawn from the German sphere of influence. Apparently this had also been intimated to the Serbian government in order to make it clear that in the event it (the Serbian government) should rebel against the German occupation forces, it would only be falling out of the frying pan into the fire.

It was already becoming increasingly evident that the hope of the Commander in Serbia for the success of the Nedić government could not be realized. Prime Minister Nedić in a radio address of September 15 exhorted insurgents to lay down their arms, cease all acts of sabotage and to maintain peace and order. "Special courts" (Sonderggerichte) would also be established for the trial of saboteurs and the administrative apparatus would be purged of unreliable officials. But as expected, this appeal had little effect.

Reports available from the middle of September speak of an expansion of the insurgent movement into Požarevac, and the growth of the revolt in Užice. The bands became especially active between Jagodina and Kragugevac. South of Belgrade our aerial reconnaissance confirmed concentrations of bands. South of Niš the bands were once more active. New centers of revolt sprang up around Višegrad, as well as west of the Drina and south of Tuzla. The inhabitants of individual Serbian villages joined the bands. The whole economy of the country fell into increasing disorder under pressure of the insurgent movement. Bands appeared on the Danube and endangered the shipping lanes, the oil supply from Rumania to the Reich. Reinforcements had to be sent to guard the Cataract Area (Iron Gate), and guards (Monitore) of the Hungarian and Rumanian Danube Flotilla had to be committed.

Until now, the newly formed Serbian Gendarmerie had been unsuccessful against the insurgents. One Gendarmerie battalion even refused to fight against the bands and another surrendered its weapons without a fight. In Šabac the Gendarmerie reinforcements could not be moved to attack the bands. The LXV Corps Command protested against a dispersed commitment of the 125th Infantry Regiment which had arrived in Belgrade, but finally acceded to the wishes of the Commander in Serbia to divert a battalion of the regiment to Šabac to disarm the unreliable Gendarmerie station there.

With the increasing numbers and strength of the bands, the pursuit detachments of 30-50 men were insufficient to combat the bands successfully, or to relieve the sentries, gendarmerie stations, and administrative sub-area headquarters encircled by the bands.

The German garrisoning divisions did not suffice even to protect the most important points. In order to remove the danger of sentry after sentry being surrounded and annihilated by the insurgents, the widely dispersed divisions linked up closer (the 718 west of the Drina, the 704 near Valjevo, the 714 near Topola and units of the 717 near Bor.

Report from Belgrade

On September 12, General Staff Major Jain, who had been sent as Liaison Officer of the General Staff to the LXV Corps Command in Belgrade, described conditions there:

"Until now operations have only been carried out with pursuit detachments, for which the divisions have been assigned pursuit areas, and the individual battalions pursuit districts. This strategy has been outdated for a long time, since the bandits have now grown to such strength that the pursuit detachments are no longer able to accomplish anything. Finally on September 6 the Corps Command issued the following order: 'The attack and destruction of any bands which appear, remains, now as before, the task of the divisions.' It was not possible to undertake such offensive action, although the 125th Infantry Regiment was available. At LXV Corps Command the opinion is unanimous that the measures used until now are insufficient to suppress the revolt. On the other hand there is little possibility of assembling a group strong enough for an attack because of the numerous, widely dispersed security tasks, entrusted to the LXV Corps Command. Moreover the Commander in Serbia had raised a protest against any troop displacement, and had reserved for himself any decision on the subject. He (Major Jain) almost had the impression that the overall view of the situation had been lost: "Here at Headquarters the opinion is that if a unit is withdrawn from a locality, the weak components which remain, will be immediately surrounded by numerous bands or destroyed. For this reason, every displacement, which also aggravates the inflexibility of the unit, has more or less ceased recently. If the situation becomes serious in any one place, at best two or three companies are raised and sent off. In this manner only a botched job is accomplished which can in no way lead to a change in the situation. At the moment the insurgents dictate measures to the offices here. This will remain the case as long as no resolve is made to go over to the offensive, at the same time giving up part of the country." Accordingly the liaison officer of the Wehrmacht Commander Southeast submitted an extensive review of the military situation in Serbia on September 12:

"In the territory of the Commander in Serbia, armed revolt is growing. The main sector of the revolt, which is spreading over the whole of the occupied territory appears to lie in the Drina bend, with the focal points at Loznica, Krupanje, in the Sava bend west of Šabac, and in the area of Obrenovac-Valjevo. The headquarters of the insurgent movement is presumed to be in huts on the slopes of the Cer mountains southwest of Šabac.

"The insurgent movement has already intensified to the extent that units under battalion strength can no longer be switched in the countryside, without running the danger of being surrounded by the insurgents in the trackless terrain. The dispatch of half battalions for the relief of encircled units only results in failure. With the appearance of a large German unit, the enemy withdraws or discards his weapons, and they reappear as harmless inhabitants of the country. Estimates of enemy strength in the Sava bend west of Šabac fluctuate between 2,000 and 10,000 men. The employment of motorized units or of individual tanks is not possible in large areas, because of the numerous (enemy) blockades on roads and paths.

"The new Serbian government of Nedić will not be in a position even with a further arming of the Serbian Gendarmerie, to suppress the revolt or to quash it completely. For this the units available are not sufficient either in number or in the type of equipment and armament. At best a suppression of the insurgent movement will only be achieved with a concentration of forces and the ruthless conduct of operations. The concentration of forces is however rendered difficult by the numerous security tasks which are set for the LXV Corps Command. To avoid yielding to the enemy the installations which have to be secured, railroads, waterways, industrial plants, etc., the units of the occupation are of necessity distributed over large areas. Therefore the creation of a mobile unit is essential for the combatting of the insurgent movement and the protecting of these installations.

The execution of the following tasks is urgent:

1) The destruction of the enemy on the Obrenovac-Valjevo road in order to re-establish a guaranteed connection between Belgrade and Valjevo.

2) The destruction of the enemy in the Sava bend west of Šabac by a concentrated thrust of strong combat troops from Šabac and Biljeljine against the Northern part of the Sava bend. For the moment the encirclement and the destruction of the headquarters of the revolt, presumed to be in the Cer, must be renounced."

On September 13:

"After the withdrawal of the two German companies from the region of Krupanje, which took place on September 6 in the face of superior insurgent forces, all of the main insurgent territory west of the Mitrovica-Šabac-Valjevo-Užice line was removed from German control. There, as in other areas in which there are no German troops, the insurgents have freedom of action. Already the enemy dictates the German counter-measure by threatening various vital points. Contrary to the previous intentions of the LXV Corps Command to commit the regiment to an attack against Valjevo a battalion of the 125th Infantry Regiment had to be posted to Šabac by order of the Commander in Serbia, in order to reinforce the security there. The fact that our forces have been attacked in the whole of the occupied area leads to the conclusion that the insurgent movement is continually growing.

"The initiative will only be snatched from the enemy by an attack of our own. The German troops, stationed in various localities for the protection of installations of the administrative sub-area and district headquarters are already partly cut off from Belgrade. If the enemy detonates more roads or sets up more ambushes, in a short time all units of the occupation troops will be cut off. The intention of the enemy to isolate the individual widely dispersed German units and to prevent the concentration of a stronger fighting forces, appears obvious.

"With the present progressive state of the insurgent movement, the dispatching of individual pursuit detachments is useless and leads to further setbacks. The reinforcing of our strongholds at especially threatened points represents only passive measures. At best this only prevents an enemy attack on the position to be protected, until the enemy feels himself one day strong enough to attack in strength. Therefore concentration for a powerful attack is absolutely necessary. Only by an opening attack on the part of the Germans, can the insurgent movement be suppressed.

"The repeated requests of Field Marshal List for reinforcements, and certainly also the impressive description of the situation by Major General Foertsch at the Fuehrer's headquarters, have caused the OKW to accept the proposals of the Wehrmacht Commander Southeast."

On the night of September 14 a radio message from Fuehrer Headquarters arrived in Athens: "OKH transfers to the Wehrmacht Commander Southeast one infantry division from France for the suppression of the unrest in Serbia." This was the 342nd Infantry Division. It proceeded to Belgrade and was subordinated to the LXV Corps Command. In addition the OKH transferred one battalion of the 100th Panzer Brigade to Belgrade and this was also subordinated to the Corps Command.

Plans for the Commitment of the 342 Division

The reinforcements which in the meantime had already arrived in Belgrade from Saloniki—the 125 Infantry Regiment and the 220 Artillery Battalion—were well-tried troops, but according to the opinion of the Commander in Serbia, they were not sufficient, even with the support of the remaining troops available, for a planned combing of the insurgent territory—plains with dense cornfields and mountains with dense forests. Therefore the Commander in Serbia wanted to confine himself at first to the commitment of the 125th Infantry Regiment from Belgrade in the direction of Obrenovac-Ub, in order to "mop up locally" and to safeguard liaison with the 704 Infantry Division in Valjevo, which had been cut off. [6]

After the arrival of the 342 Infantry Division the commander in Serbia intended to assemble a strong group to attack the insurgents in the area north of the Šabac-Loznica line. The Wehrmacht Commander Southeast also gave the order to annihilate the insurgents in the area of the Trupenje-Sava-Drina triangle. For this purpose, strong forces—at least two divisions—from Obrenovac-Ub and above all from

Valjevo were to be committed here with the object of "encircling the insurgents in the Sava-Drina triangle."[7] The 718th Infantry Division in Bosnia, reinforced by Croatian forces, was to prevent the movement of the insurgents on Croatian territory to the west bank of the Drina. The security of the Croatian territory could be effected partly by the two battalions already there, and also by the three additional Regional Defense Battalions promised for September by the OKH. After the arrival of these battalions the 718th Infantry Division would be free for the security, observation and sealing off of the Drina triangle. The Croatian Marshal Kvaternik declared himself ready to make available for the operation, "at least 12 and if possible even more Croatian battalions," whose fitness for action must first be proven. The Marshal offered to subordinate these troops to the Commander of the 718th Infantry Division. He especially desired that these Croatian battalions be used with German troops wherever possible. In view of his experiences in World War I (Fall 1914: Campaign against Serbia), he thought it practical to commence the attack of the 342 Infantry Division from Syrmia. The railroad network of Syrmia, the road network between the Drina and Kolubara, the freedom in the rear and (available) reinforcements were all in favour of this. The German General in Zagreb Brigadier General von Glaise Horstenau shared this opinion. The Croatian Government agreed to the disembarking of troops in Syrmia, and Marshal Kvaternick agreed "to make himself, the Croatian armed forces and the Croatian authorities available in every respect."[8]

On September 16 the liaison officer of the Wehrmacht Commander Southeast, General Staff Major Jain also transmitted a detailed plan for the commitment of the 342 Infantry Division, as follows:

"According to enemy reports already received, the insurgent movement seems to have made most progress in and south of the Sava bend. There the armed revolt is being planned according to a military pattern under the command of former Serbian officers. The command headquarters of the movement is supposedly in the Cer mountains. After the arrival of the 342 Infantry Division I consider an attack against this main insurgent territory especially effective for the suppression of the insurgent movement.

"The previous alarming reports concerning bands in the region south of Belgrade have proved to be very exaggerated. In contrast to the reported militarily organized bands in and to the south of the Sava bend, it appears only to have been a matter of individual sabotage units south of Belgrade. For this reason and in view of the strong garrison in the city, I see no danger for Belgrade. Therefore, with the arrival of the 342nd Infantry Division I propose the encirclement of the headquarters of the revolt which is reportedly on the Cer. Execution: disembarking of the 342nd Infantry Division provisionally about September 19 north of the Sava in the area of Šid-Mitrovica-Ruma-Klanak.

"After the disembarkation, the following assembly of the division is to be effected: Two reinforced groups of infantry regiments in the region of Mitrovica and one reinforced group of infantry regiments in the region of Klanak. The 125th Infantry Regiment reinforced by the II Battalion of the 724th Infantry Regiment, a platoon of tanks of the 220th Panzerjaeger Battalion, the 220th Artillery Battalion and two batteries of the 654th Artillery Battalion move in a three day march into the region of Loznica in order to seal off the region of the Cer Mountains from the south. The reinforced group of infantry regiments of the 342, to be assembled east of Šabac, moves in good time via Šabac into the region of Riberica in order to seal off the through traffic from northwest to southeast and vice versa. The two reinforced groups of infantry regiments assembling in the vicinity of Mitrovica, cross the Sava there and attack—one day after the crossing of the Sava by the reinforced group of infantry regiments near Šabac—the Cer Mountains in a southerly direction, in order to destroy any bands that may appear or to drive them back to the Cer Mountains.

At the same time all localities are to be searched systematically for insurgents and weapons by both the reinforced groups of infantry regiments. If the enemy offers no resistance, both reinforced groups of infantry regiments should reach the line of Prnjavor-Ribari-Lipolist-Dobric-Varna on the fourth day after the crossing of the Sava. With this line the pocket around the Cer Mountains is closed except for the Drina side.

The assistance of the Croats for the sealing off of the Drina is to be secured. After the sealing off of the pocket around the Cer Mountains the pocket is to be made narrower in the direction of the forest area by a concentrated advance, and after the edge of the forest has been reached the forest area is to be thoroughly patrolled with strong mopping-up detachments."

On September 17 the Commander in Serbia gave the following instructions to the LXV Corps Command for the operation:

"The situation in Serbia demands a German military success. The German troops at present on hand offer no expectations for the successful execution of an operation in a range of wooded hills, even after bringing in the present divisions accompanied by 30 tanks. In contrast, success will certainly be achieved in the plain region with the troops which will be available shortly. Therefore the Corps Command is commissioned to carry out as soon as possible an operation against the Sava-Drina bend in the area of Mitrovica-Šabac-northern edge of the Cer mountain range, with the units on hand and the 342 Infantry regiment which is at present on the move, and the 30 tanks of the 100th Panzer Brigade. The aim of the operation is to destroy the enemy forces established there, to re-establish orderly conditions acceptable to the German Wehrmacht, and to re-acquire this fertile region for its food supply.

"In the opinion of the Commander in Serbia, an attack with the main forces in a north-south direction on both sides of Mitrovica-to the Cer mountain range promises little expectation of success. With the news of our troop concentratin, the insurgents will most likely withdraw from the area which is to be mopped up into the wooded mountain range to the south, and at the end of the operation, after withdrawal of the majority of the troops, the insurgents will soon re-establish present conditions.

"In contrast an operation with the main thrust from the east via Šabac-Lipolist and at the same time from the west towards Janje-Bijeljina in the direction of Lipolst appears more promising. When the spearheads of the assault groups make contact in the region around Lipolst, it will be possible to seal off the plain in the direction of the Cer Mountains. The assault groups would then have to carry out the combing of the Sava-Drina bend on a broad front from south to north. To prevent the insurgents from crossing over to Croatian territory, every effort must be made to effect co-operation of the Croatian troops operating alongside the German troops (718 Infantry Division). The greatest secrecy and the surprise execution of the operation as well as the unnoticed safeguarding of the crossing of the western column over the Drina, from the region of Janje-Bijeljina towards the east, are decisive factors for success. Numerous rumours are already current in Belgrade concerning a large-scale counter-attack on the part of the German troops.

"The Wehrmacht Commander Southeast agrees to this plan of the Commander in Serbia for the operation in Northwest Serbia."

Regulation of command in Serbia

In the meantime, on September 16 the Military Administrative Councillor of State, Turner as representative of the Commander in Serbia, reported personally to Field Marshal List at his headquarters on the situation in Serbia. The description by Dr. Turner of the conditions in Serbia strengrhened the Wehrmacht Commander Southeast in his belief that "the strictest unified command" was necessary there.

In his telegram of the evening of September 17 to the OKW, he therefore repeated his proposal, to transfer to the Commanding General of the XVIII Infantry Corps, General of the Infantry Boehme, "the exclusive executive power, and to subordinate to him until further notice all military and civilian headquarters committed in Serbia" and added:

"The position of the Commander in Serbia in itself will be superfluous until the restoration of orderly conditions. Until then every special military channel must discontinue. This produces false impressions, arising continually from one-sided prerequisites, prejudices the essential unified command and endangers the overall economy." At the end of his telegram the Field Marshal stressed: "The expected speedy arrival of reinforcements, the need for a prompt pacification and restoration of the economy necessitate a decision.[9]

The telegram of the Field Marshal crossed with a Fuehrer order of September 16, excerpts of which were transmitted to the Commander Southeast by the OKW on September 17. The Fuehrer charged Field Marshal List with the task of suppressing the insurgent movement in the Southeast. For the implementation of this task, all troops already in the insurgent territory or any still to arrive were to be subordinated to the authority of the Commanding General of the XVIII Infantry Corps, General of the Infantry Boehme who would exercise executive authority in the insurgent territory. All military and civilian headquarters were to be subjected to his directives.[10]

The Fuehrer decree instructed German missions in Serbia, Roma and Zagreb:

"The driving force, organization and supplier of weapons provoking the serious and politically undesirable unrest and armed revolt in Serbia come from outside Serbia's frontiers, allowing the Serbian population no peace. In the main these are Communist and Jewish circles. Signs are present that the revolts in Serbia are instigated and supported from Bulgaria and Bulgarian Communists as well as the Russian Embassy in Sofia.

The Reich government has now resolved to strengthen the German military forces in Serbia to such an extent, that within a short time co-operation with loyal Serbian circles will be possible, the insurgents will be destroyed and disarmed and security will be re-established. If this success is not to be merely momentary, it is necessary that alliances beyond the Serbian border be located, paralyzed and rendered harmless. This can only be achieved in close co-operation with the bordering states, especially Bulgaria. The Reich Foreign Minister therefore requests that the Bulgarian government be informed of this

attitude, and that its active co-operation with the German government be requested." The Reich Foreign Minister had no doubt that
he need only make this appeal in order to receive the assent of the
Bulgarian government. A similar request would be made to the Italian
government and to the Croatian government.

On September 18 the Commanding General of the XVIII Infantry
Corps, General of Infantry Boehme arrived in Belgrade from Athens
with his staff prompting a critical examination of the insurgent movement by the Ic department of the Plenipotentiary Commanding
General in Serbia.

"The insurgent movement in Serbia is being supported by Četnik
units and Communist bands. At the moment the Četnik units are
split into three groups: the units of Kosta Pećanac, standing behind
the Nedić government; the groups of General Novaković who is inclined towards the Communists; and the anti-communist units of
Colonel of the General Staff Colonel Mihailović.

"Mihailović is opposed to Pećanac and Novaković. His circle of
followers comprises mostly officers and his organization is drawn up
on purely military lines. He rejects communism, does not feel the
time is ripe for a general revolt, and he wants to organize the whole
territory and then attack.

"The communist bands possess a centralized military and political
leadership. The main areas of activity of the communist bands are:
the territory around Bor, the Joilica mountain range, and the area of
Čačak-Arilje-Ivanjica. The Goljica mountain range is a purely Četnik
area which the Četniks and the mountain peasants rule as masters,
allow no one to enter, and recruit men into their forces. In the whole
west zone of Serbia, from Syrmian-Mitrovica in the north to Užice
in the south, no clear separation is possible between the Četniks and
panslavistic communist bands. This zone is partially under the domi-
nation of the bands."[11]

Very shortly after his arrival in Belgrade, the Plenipotentiary
Commanding General had also gained the impression that Communists and Nationalists (i.e., Mihailović Četniks—*author*) were
working together. "The Command lies" General of Infantry Boehme
reported to Field Marshal List on September 25, "in the hands of
Serbian officers. There seems to be a sufficient number of both men
and military commanders; weapons, reportedly including artillery,
are brought out of their hiding places by the insurgents, a few of
which have been procured by attacks on German troops and Serbian
gendarmerie. The enemy has also increased its limited troops and

weapons through defections from Serbian gendarmerie. Training is continually carried out by the bands and they also hold regulation firing practice. Organizing is certainly not yet finished. A great danger exists in this respect that captured enemy weapons and ammunition which lie in the central and southwestern part of the country, are especially exposed to the danger of an enemy attack.

"The Nedić government is not succeeding. On many occasions it has acted energetically against the Communists, and has also opposed the insurgent Nationalists. It is certain that Nedić has not succeeded in obtaining the support of the 1200 Serbian officers who are supposed to be in Belgrade. Scarcely 100 have placed themselves at his disposal. It has also been confirmed that one of the best insurgent commanders, Colonel Mihailović has made contact with Serbian officers in Belgrade. Nedić has also not succeeded in raising the 5,000 men which were permitted him for the reinforcement of his Gendarmerie; only 1,100 have placed themselves at his disposal. Colonel Mihailović is also supposed to have his feelers in the Serbian police.

"Nevertheless I think it best not to alienate Nedić from us, since he still has some adherents, especially in Belgrade and in the southern part of the country (Kosta Pečanac). The attacks of the foreign press against Nedić proves that he does not work in the interest of our enemy, and that he must have forces behind him.

"The situation which has now arisen proves decisively that we have regarded conditions far too patiently and too optimistically and that the situation had been completely misjudged. The false belief still existed that it was a question of a communist movement in the land and that a Nedić government would bring about a purge." "A misjudgment of the situation," continued Infantry General Boehme, "is indicated also by the completely insufficient security of Belgrade, the further reinforcement of the Serbian Gendarmerie, the removal of a leave prohibition for the troops, a carefully regulated transfer of captured enemy weapons and ammunition from the territories which are especially endangered." For all these reasons he considered the immediate recall of the Commander in Serbia necessary. This would also simplifiy at the moment the co-operation which was so imperative between him and the previous staff of the Commander in Serbia.

The report made by Infantry General Boehme caused the Wehrmacht Commander Southeast to propose to the OKW, that the Commander in Serbia be relieved. Accordingly it, the OKW, arranged for the recall of Air Corps General Dankelmann on October 8.

2. The Progress of the Mopping Up Operations in Northwest Serbia in the Sava-Drina-Valjevo area

Mid-September to End of October 1941

Thrust of the 125th Infantry Regiment towards Valjevo

On September 15, three days before Infantry General Boehme took over command in Serbia, the 125th Infantry Regiment, reinforced by one artillery battalion, one platoon of captured enemy tanks and one railway armoured train departed from Belgrade, to mop up the insurgent territory west and southwest of Belgrade, and to re-establish contact with the staff of the 704 Infantry Division, which was encircled in Valjevo. On the 17th the regiment arrived at Obrenovac, on the next day it mopped up south of this town, arrived at Ub on the 19th without any combat worth mentioning, and marched into Valjevo on the 21st without meeting with any resistance. In the following days the 125th Infantry Regiment mopped up the vicinity of this band-infested town.

Operations of the 342nd Infantry Division in the Mačva

At the time when the 125th Infantry Regiment was pushing forward from Belgrade to Valjevo, the 342nd Infantry Division disembarked on the Syrmia-Mitrovica-Klanak area for the purpose of first mopping up the territory north of the Cer mountain range in the Drina-Sava bend, of taking away from the insurgents the fertile Mačva as a provisioning base, and through the pacification of this area, of preventing a threat to the important railroad line between Zagreb-Belgrade.

On September 28 the 342nd Infantry Division, reinforced by the I Battalion of the 202nd Panzer Jaeger Regiment fell in for the first major operation with the main point of attack towards Šabac. The division was hindered in its advance by numerous road blocks, but met scarcely any resistance. The insurgents had already evacuated the Drina-Sava bend at the commencement of the deployment of the 342nd Infantry Regiment, and had withdrawn towards the southwest into the mountains.

A week after the commencement of the operation by the 342nd Infantry Division, the situation in Serbia had not changed. In all areas, with the exception of the Banat and the area south of Niš (here the Pečanac adherents had the upper hand), unrest continued to reign. Surprise attacks occurred on German security battalions, Serbian gendarmerie stations and acts of sabotage on industrial works, railroad installations, telephone lines, etc.

The march of the 125th Infantry Regiment from Belgrade to Valjevo brought no pacification of this area. The insurgent wave closed up again at the rear of the regiment. The operation of the 342nd Infantry Division was also unsuccessful, because an encirclement was not achieved. The insurgents had already fallen back before the division arrived. A total of 1,000 killed and 14,000 prisoners was reported during the mopping up of the Drina-Sava bend and the northern edge of the Cer Mountains. Only a small number of insurgents were captured and hardly any weapons were seized. The 342nd Infantry Division should not have advanced direct from the north over the Drina into the Mačva, but should have taken the insurgents in a pincer movement from west to east, north of the Cer Mountains, together with the 125th Infantry Regiment which had been diverted from Valjevo. But the anxiety in the Cer mountain range where the insurgents were gathering had a restraining effect and led to an abortive attack by the troops.

Review of the situation by the Chief of the General Staff, Wehrmacht Commander Southeast

"It is doubtful," wrote Major General Foertsch in a report, "whether a concentrated attack (the 342 Infantry Division with the 125 Infantry Regiment) would have produced a better result, since already before the entry of the troops, the insurgents had fallen back." Their mobility [on foot, no vehicles, no packs] made such a falling back easy for them. For this reason the aim of the insurgents is not to hold a particular area, or to defend it against German troops, but surprise attacks and [to create] general unrest. This is a decisive point. We do not have to deal with an enemy who is militarily organized and equipped, who therefore has great freedom of movement, and is not thrown back on particular provisioning bases (thus the intention of taking the 'provisioning bases' away from the enemy who fights according to the general rules of warfare. The enemy is also not easily recognized from his outward appearance. The peasant who appears peaceful as the troops march through, may have fought armed an hour previously, and after the troops have passed through will fight again. The retreat of such an enemy or his fleeing out of the area to be mopped up can only be prevented if the troops concentrically comb the area very thoroughly before the first attack. For this, strong units are necessary, or the area to be mopped up must be relatively small corresponding to the weakness of our troops. The active mobile units which are at our disposal are much too weak in comparison to the extensive insurgent territory."

The Chief of the General Staff examined the question of whether a further thrust of the 342nd Infantry Division into the mountains would have brought success. He had to give a negative reply, because the 342nd Infantry Division was insufficiently committed, and the insurgents could only be destroyed if they were tightly enveloped, or if the possibility existed of driving them against a fixed obstruction and of intercepting them there.

The answers to the following questions were decisive for the continuation of the fight as far as the Chief of the General Staff was concerned.

What do we want?

What can we accomplish?

What must we do therefore?

He reasoned as follows:

"We do not wish to retain Serbia as part of the Reich and for that reason to pacify it, in the manner of the Protectorate or Poland. We want to extract as many economic advantages as possible from the country. Above all we want to safeguard communication between the Reich and Balkans for provisioning, for the transportation of economic materials and for any deployment movements which may become necessary.

"Our ability depends on our own forces and the tactics of the enemy. Our own forces are limited. The bringing of the expected second combat division cannot take place if at all, before the middle of November. Therefore we cannot pacify the whole of Serbia at one time, i.e., to destroy all the insurgents at the same time. We can only mop up and secure a limited area in successive actions.

"Therefore we must at first limit ourselves to the area which is most important for us. This area is the region between the Danube and a line which runs from north to south in such a manner that the Belgrade-Niš-Skoplje railroad, and the Belgrade-Niš highway to Bulgaria and Macedonia, as well as the parallel axis of signal communication, remains secured. Therefore, it is a question of establishing peace and safety, in an absolute sense, in this "German Corridor," by giving up, for the time being, that Serbian territory which lies southwest of such a line.

"A concentrating of troops in this corridor runs the danger that at first the insurgents will have freedom of action in the mountainous terrain southwest of this corridor, and thereby will be able to improve their organization, armament and equipment. This danger must be taken into consideration for a certain period of time. It will only be lessened by the fact that this area will be stripped of all stocks, of foodstuffs (cattle, grain) to the greatest possible extent, by the evacuating troops, and that a further policing by the Luftwaffe and destruction by bomb attacks and possibly also by tank thrusts will take place. Such tank thrusts however may not weaken to any extent the forces which are necessary for the mopping up of the corridor. The southwest limit of the corridor must be secured in such a way that a thrust into it by the insurgents cannot take place. (Blockades by means of entanglements, mines and watchtowers)(?) (*original illegible here*)

Proposal for the continuation of the fight against the insurgents

General Foertsch proposed therefore:

"To concentrate the 704 and the 717th Infantry Divisions in such a manner, that the above-mentioned channels of communication (railroad, highway, axis of signal communication) are finally effectively secured.

"To break off the operation of the 342nd Infantry Division which had been in effect since 9.28 and to commit the division, together with the 125th Infantry Regiment and the forces situated in and around Belgrade, to the mopping up of the area south of Belgrade, in such a manner, that the insurgents there would be encircled or would be pressed against the Danube east of Belgrade and would be intercepted there.

"Thereafter to commit the 342nd Infantry Division and the 125th Infantry Regiment for the mopping up of the territory southwest of Ternu Severin in such a manner, that the insurgents of this area will be ejected from the southwest and west to the northeast and north in the direction of the Danube." "To mop up the 'German Corridor' in similar actions in the course of time." "To employ the troops for combatting the insurgents outside of this corridor until the end of this mopping up action.

"From the completely secured Corridor, concentrated as a jumping-off base, to operate patrol platoons, reinforced by tank units, in the southwest Serbian territory, in order to rout the insurgents or to encircle them. These patrol platoons can at the same time be set up as marauding expeditions, in order at the same time to make life as difficult for the insurgents by confiscating foodstuffs, destruction, etc., as the insurgents at the present time make it for us.

"To proceed with a final pacification and mopping up of this southwest mountain range only after the importation of further active combat forces."[12]

Thrust of the 342nd Infantry Division on Krupanj

Field Marshal List turned down these proposals in this exaggerated form because according to his observations, too much freedom would be given to the insurgents for the organization of further powerful units. So the 342nd Infantry Division continued the operation. On the morning of October 10 the division fell in once more for the fighting against the insurgents. The division was committed, with three regimental groups from the north and somewhat weaker forces from the southwest, for the destruction of rather strong bands north of the Jader, in the Cer and Iverak mountain ranges.

The spearhead of the 342nd Infantry Division reached Loznice and the district south of it by the 11th, liberating 40 wounded German soldiers in and around Loznica held captive by the bandits. While the division in the following days mopped up the Cer and Iverak mountain ranges, the forward units advanced on Krupanj meeting strong enemy resistance south of the Jader. In addition the continuation of the operation was hindered by heavy rainfall. The division reorganized itself south of the Cer mountain range for an attack on Krupanj.

On October 20 the 342nd Infantry Division fell upon Krupanj, and on the same day occupied this town in the face of weak enemy resistance. The insurgents had put up, on the whole, no considerable resistance against the 342nd Infantry Division, after the breaking of the resistance south of the Jader and had retreated en masse from the district of Krupanj towards the south and southwest.

One gun and 2 machine guns were captured during this operation. The losses of the 342nd Infantry Division consisted of 10 dead and 44 wounded, while the Serbian losses were considerable, 1,800 dead.

Mopping up of the Kolubara territory by the 125th Infantry Regiment

In the rear of the 125th Infantry Regiment the revolt had broken out once again. Therefore in the second week of October, the regiment had to be committed once more, from Valjevo towards the north, to mop up the territory of Kolubara (Lajkovac-Ub-Obrenovac). The regiment was hindered on its march to Obrenovac by road blocks and demolitions. While the staff of the regiment and one battalion arrived in Obrenovac on October 13, a reinforced battalion of the regiment fought against the enemy armed with machine guns in the vicinity of Stopojevac. On the 17th peace was once more restored to the area of Kraljeva. As reprisal for the sudden attack on this town 1,736 men and 19 women were shot.

The III Battalion of the 749th Infantry Regiment had to be sent again from Kragujevac to G. Milanovac to carry out reprisal measures. After a successful engagement with bands, the regiment returned to Kragujevac with 100 hostages. Severe measures had to be taken to re-establish peace in this insurgent area. In all a total of 529 bandits were killed, and all localities on the road and the Kruševac-Kraljevo-Čačak-Valjevo railroad line were depopulated.

Estimate of the situation by the Plenipotentiary Commanding General in Serbia

The severe attacks of the German Wehrmacht, especially the ruthlessly executed reprisal measures seemed to have led to a sobering up of at least a part of the Serbian population by the end of October. According to a report of 10.30.41 of the Plenipotentiary Commanding General in Serbia a total of 3,853 Serbs were arrested. In Belgrade 405 hostages were shot (until now a total of 4,750), 90 Communists in Šabac, 2,300 hostages in Kragujevac, and 1,700 in Kraljevo. The prison camp at Šabac on October 15 contained 16,545 Serbs. In the area south of Obrenovac, which the 125th Infantry had mopped up, the inhabitants of individual villages had joined together for the purpose of self-defense against the Communists and brought information about the enemy to the German units. Reports about signs of resistance by the population against the Communist terror were also received from the district of Kruševac and east of Valjevo. In the district of Obrenovac, 70 insurgents surrendered and handed over their weapons to the Serbian gendarmerie. In the district of Paraćin a Četnik detachment deserted to Pećanac.

In the second half of October, the Serbian Auxiliary Gendarmerie carried out about 16 major police operations, during which the enemy lost about 377 dead, 19 wounded and 108 prisoners. During these engagements the Serbian Gendarmerie captured some weapons. Četniks, loyal to the government, also fought against the Communist bands and suffered losses.

It was probable that the majority of the Račić-Četniks which had appeared in the northwest parts of Serbia had withdrawn before the 342nd Infantry Division across the Drina towards East Bosnia, and had reinforced there the Četnik groups of Dangić. Units of the Račić-Četniks may also have withdrawn to the southeast, into the main assembly area of the Mihailović units, the district between the upper western Morava and Kolubara. It was presumed however that weak units of the Račić-Četniks were still in the area around Krupanj.

As captured documents show, strong signs of disintegration appeared among the partisan units (Communists) during and after the attack of the 342nd Infantry Division. It was certain that many units, especially the forcefully conscripted ones, had given up band activity and now attempted to return to the north into the Sava-Drina bend and to disappear. "It may however be supposed," the Plenipotentiary Commanding General in Serbia judged, "that the partisans in this area are destroyed. Attempts at reorganization are probable. Wherever there are no troops, small bands will continue to terrorize and carry out acts of sabotage."

The enemy continued to hold the Dobrava section southeast of Šabac, and appeared to receive reinforcements from the east. It must be presumed that a strong enemy group, at least 2,000 men was in the area southeast of Šabac. As a result of the mopping up operations of the 125th Infantry Regiment, signs similar to these among the Communists in the northwest, appeared in the area southeast of Obrenovac. From captured documents it can be seen that at the very beginning of the fight, half of a strong partisan unit fled, but again reappeared. The bands continued to keep Kraljevo encircled and since October 30 have renewed their attack on this town.

South of the Danube, Dl. Milanova was seized by a strong band after the withdrawal of German troops. However, without disturbing the shipping, the bands withdrew again towards Maidanpek, where they were dispersed by the II Battalion of the 741st Infantry Regiment. Traffic on the Danube continued without interruption. Cases of sabotage on the railroads and highways of the main communication line Belgrad-Niš had decreased at the end of October. Considerable sabotage on economic installations was reported from the district of Draževac. On October 20 production began again in the copper mines at Bor.

Intentions of the Plenipotentiary Commanding General in Serbia

On October 21 the OKH informed the Wehrmacht Commander Southeast, that the 113th Infantry Division would be sent as reinforcement instead of the 99th Light Division as previously intended. The Plenipotentiary Commanding General in Serbia, General of Infantry Boehme, now intended to carry out the destruction of the enemy, located to the south of the Dobrava sector, by means of a concentric attack from Ub, Valjevo, Šabac and Obrenovac with the 342nd Infantry Division. He planned to commit the newly approaching 113th Infantry Division for an attack from the area of Jagodina-Kruševac via Kragujevac, Gorni Milanovac and via Kraljevo-Čačak for the purpose of regaining the western area Morava.[13]

3. Continuation of the Fight with the Insurgents, November 1941

On the afternoon of October 26, General of Engineers Kuntze, who had been the Commanding General of the XXXXII Infantry Corps, now became the representative of the ailing Field Marshal List, and also acted as deputy commander of the 12th Army. He arrived at the air field of Tatoi, and the following day assumed command. In the final days of October (27-31) the staff of the Wehrmacht Commander Southeast transferred from Kopfissia to Salonika. The operational department was quartered in Arsakli. In the coming months, the combatting of the insurgent movement in Serbia and Bosnia remained the most decisive and demanding activity of the Wehrmacht Commander Southeast, in addition to numerous other tasks—defense problems in Greece and on the island of Crete, the setting up of the Fortress Division Crete, difficult transport and supply matters, etc.

New fighting of the 342nd Infantry Division near Šabac and Valjevo

Clashes with the insurgents in Serbia continued in November. At the beginning of this month a total of nine battalions—the 342nd Infantry Division and the I and II Battalions of the 125th Infantry Regiment[14] were committed to the destruction of strong bands which were reported southeast of Šabac on the Dobrava sector-Dobric-Banjani and north of Valjevo near Koceljevo. The I and II Battalions of the 697th Infantry Regiment and the I Battalion of the 125th Infantry Regiment advanced from the area between Banjani and the Sava towards the west, while the III Battalion of the 697th Infantry Regiment and the III Battalion of the 125th Infantry Regiment closed the front towards the east on the Dobrava sector. Other units of the 342nd Infantry Regiment—four battalions—joined the 5th from the area of Koceljevo towards the southwest. The main body of the enemy however fell back before this attack to the southwest. The 699th Infantry Regiment only made contact with an enemy group on the 7th in the Koceljevo-Kamenica-Valjevo triangle. This operation was concluded on the 9th southeast of Šabac and south of Koceljevo. In these clashes the insurgents suffered great losses, at least 100 dead. In addition 130 hostages were shot in reprisal. On the 11th the units of the 342nd Infantry Division returned to their quarters in Valjevo.

It is apparent that the commitment of the 342nd Infantry Division and of the 125th Infantry Regiment in the area southwest of Šabac and the recently concluded push from Kraljevo-Koceljevo have not led to the complete destruction of the insurgents. However the bands in the northwest area of Serbia had been dispersed. It was obvious that they had suffered a severe blow. Signs of disintegration appeared within the bands. The local population which up until now had been oppressed by the bands, welcomed our troops in many places and requested their protection. Near Loznica on the 13th a fight flared up for the first time between the units of Mihailović and Communist bands. The III Battalion of the 697th Infantry Regiment was quickly transferred from Lesnica to Loznica for the protection of the antimony works at Zaječar (Krupanje). On the 15th Loznica was taken. A large number of Mihailović Četniks were taken prisoner here. Weapons (rifles, machine guns, mortars and hand grenades) as well as a large amount of infantry ammunition (10,000 rounds) were captured. From the new quarters the battalion developed an extremely lively reconnaissance and combat activity. Weak partisan groups withdrew from the Cer Mountains and the Vardar Valley to the southeast.

At the same time engagements of the 342nd Infantry Regiment were repeated in the area of Valjevo—engagements which lasted until the end of November. Here again, and around November 20, the area of Lesnica also had to be mopped up of bands which appeared again. Occasionally bitter fights occurred with Communist bands, who had to be destroyed in close combat in improved field positions.

Mopping up operations of the 717th and 718th Infantry Divisions

Strong Communist groups have appeared in the upper valley of the Western Morava. Here the fights again flared up around Kraljevo which the insurgents unsuccessfully attacked again without artillery on October 31. Numerous operations, many of them causing the enemy heavy losses, were carried out by the 717th Infantry Division in the area of Western Morava. During a thrust of the 749th Infantry Regiment, from Kraljevo towards the south, up the Ibar Valley in the direction of Raška, where a communist group had also appeared, an enemy rearguard was thrown back near Bogutovac. Numerous road blockades were removed. Further mopping up operations of German units, in conjunction with the Serbian gendarmerie, as well as with the support of Pećanac adherents, continued against communist bands in the Morava Valley until the end of November. The bands also had to be driven from their hide-outs in the mountains and woods south of Kragujevac. However the Western Morava Valley remained in the possession of the Communists. Užice, where the "main headquarters of the Commander of all the Partisan Units of Serbia" was situated, was the center of this insurgent movement. In spite of two bombing attacks by our Luftwaffe, the armament factory at Užice continued to work for the insurgents.

In the northeastern area of Serbia, during November, units of the 714th Infantry Division were occupied with numerous small mopping up operations, during which they were often supported by the Serbian auxiliary gendarmerie. Obrenovac, Lazarevac, Arandjelovac, Pozarevac, V. Plana, Jagodina, Kragujevac, Paračin, Zajecar, Negotin and Petrovac were the scenes of local fights. A large scale operation of the Serbian auxiliary gendarmerie near Požarevac was supported by the II Battalion of the 721st Infantry Regiment and by tanks. German river guards and half of the Hungarian Danube flotilla were also committed to box in the insurgents. Units of the 704th Infantry Division which had been transferred from the Banat to the area of Valjevo, were brought up in the middle of November to Pozarevac, where the division staff was also posted.

Another large-scale operation of the 714th Infantry Division was carried out around the middle of November with one battalion each of the 721st, 724th and 741st Infantry Regiments northeast of Kragujevac.

Estimate of the situation middle of November

The II Battalion of the 125th Infantry Regiment which had remained in Belgrade again pacified the district south of the city and around Ripanj of small communist bands at the beginning of November. In Belgrade itself and in the Banat peace reigned. In the remaining Serbian area the situation was still characterized by scattered band attacks. The area of sabotage acts and surprise attacks had moved around the middle of November more and more to the southeast. New bands appeared in large numbers near Aleksinac, Leskovac, Prakuplje, and above all around Niš-Pirot. As the Plenipotentiary Commanding General in Serbia reported, the resistance of the Serbian population against the insurgents, especially in the southern part of the country, was growing. The Serbian government, with its auxiliary gendarmerie seemed now to have consolidated itself.

The increased attacks on the Niš-Pirot, and Niš-Skoplje railroad caused the reinforcement of Bulgarian railroad security by two more Bulgarian battalions. The transport situation was critical, not only because of a lack of usable locomotives, but also because of the numerous interruptions of operations by sabotage acts. From November 5 the first echelons of the 113rd Infantry Division approached via

Syrmia. In consideration of the importance of the securing of the Zagreb-Belgrade railroad, the Wehrmacht Commander Southeast instructed the Plenipotentiary Commanding General in Serbia on November 13, to examine whether and how railroad security could be reinforced. It was planned to protect in a better manner the main line Belgrade-Niš-Skoplje by means of a fortified defense system (watchtowers).

Thanks to the energetic attacks of our troops,[15] and also due to the approaching winter—in the middle of November snowstorms were common in north and central Serbia, and frost had set in—the acts of sabotage and the surprise attacks had in general decreased. In the coming spring a revival of the insurgent movement and increased surprise attacks can be expected. The Wehrmacht Commander Southeast therefore considered—as he had already informed the OKW and the OKH on November 14—that in addition to the 113th Infantry Division the dispatch of a further division to Serbia, and a division to Croatia, where the situation worsened, was necessary in the coming months. He also considered the dispatch of a further division to Salonika around the middle of January as desirable, in order to replace the 16th Infantry Division, which together with units of the 713th Infantry Division and the 125th Infantry Regiment, was intended for the formation of the "Fortress Division Crete," which was about to be organized. The 125th Infantry Regiment and the 3rd Company of the 220th Panzer-Jaeger Battalion were withdrawn from Serbia around the end of November. The 125th Infantry Regiment was to be transferred as soon as possible to Crete in order to relieve the 5th Mountain Division there, which was intended for commitment in the East.

The offer of Mihailović to care for weapons

As already mentioned, bloody combats occurred for the first time between Mihailović units and communist bands about the 11th of November near Loznica. Bitter struggles also occurred between battalions of Draža Mihailović and communist bands for the possession of Užice, Požega, Čačak, Grn. Milanovac, and also southeast of Valjevo and south of Lazarevac. Above all it was a matter of "a fight for the food bases between the individual bands."[16] Be that as it may, Mihailović seemed to be serious in his struggle against the Communists.

About the middle of November, Draža Mihailović, the most influential leader of the national Serbian insurgent movement, made an offer through his intermediary to the Plenipotentiary Commanding General in Serbia, to fight with his bands together with the German troops against the Communists. For this purpose he demanded weapons for his Četniks.[17] As the Wehrmacht Commander Southeast wired to the OKW on November 13 in reply to an inquiry, this offer was turned down and unconditional surrender was demanded. An answer has not yet been received. A fight took place yesterday for the first time between Mihailović bands and Communists. This fact however did not alter the German demand for unconditional surrender which Mihailović did not answer. On the occasion of the setting up of the 'Battalion of a Serbian Mountain Brigade,' he immediately sent an envoy to King Peter with the request for an early return to Yugoslavia. [18]

On November 12 the Rudnik agency in Belgrade published the following explanation of the Minister President, Milan Nedić, concerning the negotiations with Mihailović:

"On Monday evening the London radio spoke about the political situation in Serbia, and thereby made the false statement that the German authorities had negotiated with Draza Mihailović. The contrary is true! Draza Mihailović sent his representative to me as well as to the German authorities in order to negotiate with them. The German authorities turned down every negotiation with his intermediary, and demanded that Mihailović himself put in an appearance and surrender unconditionally.

"In this respect I confirm that when I took over the government, tried to unite under my command all national Serbian circles for the salvation of Serbia in order to spare Serbian blood, and to this end I negotiated with Kòsta Pečanac as well as with Mihailović. Kosta Pečanac possessed so much love for his fatherland, that he immediately declared himself ready to fall in with my wishes. Draza Mihailović, on the contrary, seemed to want to obtain money from me, and then collaborated with the Communists. I even have proof that he made written agreements with them. If Radio London now works for Mihailović, it is the best proof that he works for Moscow and the Communists on English instruction. For this reason the German Wehrmacht gave him the answer that such a man deserves. As far as we Serbs are concerned, he is as much an enemy as any Communist because of those actions." Thus in the course of the month of November the situation in Serbia had not changed substantially. The pacification in the north of the country had indeed made progress, the economy was being restored again here and there, but in the main insurgent territory of the Western Morava area the insurgents continued to fight against the German occupation troops, although they were opposed to each other. Therefore at the end of November the Wehrmacht Commander Southeast planned to carry out the final mopping up of the territory of Western Morava and the territory north of it after the arrival of the 113th Infantry Division was complete by the advance of this division from the line Jagodina-Kruševac to the west, while the 342nd Infantry Division was to advance at the same time from the area of Valjevo towards the southeast. [19]

Protection of the armaments industry in Old Serbia; the most urgent task

Then the Wehrmacht Commander Southeast received a new directive from the OKW. On November 16 the OKW communicated the basic principles of an order concerning the armaments industry in Old Serbia. According to this directive the protection of the most important metal and coal mines and armaments plants was designated as the most urgent task. [20] This meant that in view of the troops available, the combatting of the insurgent movement must recede into the background.

At the moment a temporary pacification of Serbia was indeed to be expected, but a revival of the insurgent movement must be reckoned with in the coming months. Therefore the Wehrmacht Commander Southeast had demanded a further increased reinforcement of forces. However, to the proposal that two further divisions be brought up for "offensive commitment" against the main insurgent territories in Serbia and Croatia, the OKW replied that no further forces could be brought to Serbia before the Spring of 1942. This meant a change in the tasks of the Wehrmacht Commander Southeast: suppression of the insurgent movement. Only then above all, could the mines and armaments industries, and the transport lines to the industrial areas be secured according to the directives of the OKW. With the forces available in Serbia, the same untenable situation could once again arise, which had prevailed before the Corps Headquarters of the XVIII Infantry Corps had taken over command in Serbia. [21]

The intention of the Wehrmacht Commander Southeast now was first to carry out the mopping up of the Western Morava territory by means of the 113rd and 342nd Infantry Divisions. An additional task would be holding the most important industrial points, then the security of transport movements through Serbia, and finally at least a local combatting of bands.

4. Combats in the Territory of Western Morava
End of November to beginning of December 1941

On November 24 the 113rd Infantry Division arrived in the area of Jagodina-Kruševac. During the deployment of the division the disembarked troops had already carried out local operations against small communist bands in the region of Paraćin and Kruševac. In the meantime the Plenipotentiary Commanding General had gained a picture of the situation in the area of Western Morava.

Mihailović, who at the moment opposed the Communists with his units and actually fought against them, was apparently pressed back towards the west by the partisan bands. Rudnick, Grn. Milanovac, Gruza, Čačak, Požega, Užice, Cajetina, Oieja, Guča and the Ibar Valley between Konarevo and Ušće were in the possession of the partisans. Furthermore a strong concentration of bands in the territory of Western Morava was confirmed. It was apparent that Communist battalions and troops from the area south of Belgrade and central Morava had moved into that area.[22]

The result of the attack on Užice

The Wehrmacht Commander Southeast, General of Engineers Kuntze had gone to Belgrade at this time (11.30 to 12.2), in order personally to conduct discussions concerning the combatting of the insurgent movement with Generals Boehme, Bader and Glaise-Horstenau. After his return to Saloniki, the Wehrmacht Commander Southeast was able to confirm the following from reports on hand:

"The operations of the 342nd and 113rd Infantry Divisions have taken the insurgents in the Užice-Cacak area by surprise. To be sure, the majority succeeded in escaping to the south and southwest into the territory of Croatia occupied by Italian troops, however insurgent losses of approximately 2,000 men, are very high. These facts, together with the arrival of winter, permit the expectation that the communist insurgent movement in the Serbian areas is to be considered as suppressed for the time being.

During the Užice operation (25 November-4 December) our troops lost a total of 11 dead and 35 wounded.

The losses of the insurgents were exceptionally high: 1,415 dead of whom 389 were shot in reprisal, 80 wounded and 718 prisoners. Booty brought in comprised: 4 guns, 3 mortars, 2,723 rifles, 8 small machine guns, 20 light machine guns, 1 tank (destroyed), 8 horse drawn vehicles, 215 horses, 23 vehicles, 6 motorcycles, 5 gliders (burnt-out) and 3 field safes containing one million dinars.

Furthermore our troops captured: 7 weapon and ammunition depots, 3 explosive dumps with a considerable quantity of artillery ammunition, numerous weapons and aircraft bombs. Especially wel-
come was the capture of 6 gasoline and ration depots containing
1,800,000 litres of gasoline and 2,000,000 litres of oil as well as
large quantities of food-stuffs, which the bandits abandoned. In
addition there were 6 other depots with signals and quartering equipment, with maps, propaganda material, and medical equipment.

In the rifle and ammunition factory in Užice approximately 400
valuable pieces of machinery of German origin, 1,500 bars of lead,
many lead pipes, antimony, nickel, tin, a large quantity of half finished goods, weapons and ammunition, templates and packing material
were captured. On the railroad Užice-Kremna-Vardište approximately (?) locomotives and 100 freight cars containing weapons, ammunition, engineering and signal equipment, machinery and rations of all
kinds.

Furthermore 20 freight cars wtih gasoline, 30 with timber and 80
with cloth were also captured.

Separation of HQ. XVIII Inf. Corps, from the Twelfth Army

On the second of December in the middle of this operation the
order of OKH arrived which called for the posting to Wehrkreis XVIII
of Corps Headquarters XVIII Infantry Corps, General of Infantry
Boehme together with the Corps troops, were ear-marked for the
eastern front. On the 6th of December General of Infantry Boehme
was relieved by General of Artillery Bader as "Plenipotentiary Commanding General in Serbia." The XVIII Infantry Corps Headquarters
was transferred from the Twelfth Army and left Belgrade within the
next few days.

Continuation of the mopping up operations

In the meantime the 342nd and the 113rd Infantry Divisions had
already received new orders for the continuation of the mopping up
operations. In the northwest area of Serbia, between Krupanje-
Valjevo and Koceljeva, between Arandjelovac and the Kosmaj Mountains, in the Morava valley south of Arilje, in the Ibar valley, north
of Novi Pazar, where the Albanians were still fighting the Serbs, and
in the territory around Leskovac, remnants of large communist
bands were still reported.

As a result of the German operations in the upper Western Morava
area, the Mihailović units were for the most part dispersed. However
remnants of this insurgent group were still probably in the area
around Rudnik and in the Babina-Glava mountains. It was important

to prevent a new consolidation of these numerous dispersed band remnants, some of which had retreated beyond the Italian demarcation line, others into Serbian territory towards the southwest and the southeast. On December 3 the 342nd Infantry Division received an order to destroy the Mihailović groups in the Babina-Glava mountains. The 113th Infantry Division was to break up the strong bands which had been reported in the Moravica vally in the region of Arilje-Ivanica and in the territories of Raška, Novi Pazar and Mitrovica.

On December 4 Ivanjica in the Moravica valley was captured. On the 7th troops of the 113th Infantry Division occupied Novi Pazar without having contact with the enemy. On the 9th the division broke up bands in the district of Arilje. In the meantime other units of the 113th and the 717th Infantry Divisions combed the areas of Užice, Požega, Čačak and Kraljevo once more and therefore caused further dispersal of band remnants.

The 342nd Division surrounded the Mihailović Četniks who were presumably southeast of Valjevo and on December 7 fell in concentrically with five battalions in the direction of Babina-Glava. Mihailović could only withdraw with difficulty from the attack of our troops. He fled with a few supporters to East Bosnia. His staff together with its Chief, Major Mišić was captured. During this operation of the 342nd Infantry Division the Mihailović Četniks lost approximately ten dead and 350 prisoners. Considerable booty was brought in by the unit: 330 rifles, 5 machine guns, 21,000 rounds of infantry ammunition, 1,100 telephones, one short wave receiver, several motorcycles, 37 horses and a field safe with 203,000 dinars.

The largest group of the national Serbian insurgents was now broken up! At the conclusion of this operation the 342nd Infantry Division returned to its bivouac area east of the Drina and south of the Sava. The III Battalion of the 697th Infantry Regiment which had remained in Loznica was once more subordinated to its division. The units of the 718th Infantry Division which were stationed in Gr. Mitovica, Šabac and Zvornik were released and posted once more to Croatia for the purpose of combatting insurgency.

Since the 27th of November the III Battalion 697th Infantry Regiment had been in combat with communist bands who threatened Krupanje. At the beginning of December this battalion had carried out successful local mopping up operations in the frontier territory on the Drina and in the Iverak and the Cer mountains, northeast of Loznica. The battalions of the divisions of the 15th Wave which were attached to the 113th Infantry Division and to the 342nd Infantry Division for the attack on Užice were returned to their old bivouac areas at the end of the operations.

5. The situation in Serbia at the end of 1941

Estimate of the situation by General of Artillery Bader

The offensive operations of the 113rd and 342nd Infantry Divisions, for the most part, were finished. They had achieved the expected success, and effected considerable pacification of the situation in Serbia.

On December 10 General of Artillery Bader reported: "The most decisive factor was not so much the number of insurgents disposed of in battle, but rather the draconic reprisal measures and the fact that sufficiently strong, superior armed and well-equipped German troops under a mobile and energetic command, sought out the bands in these positions, where they had thought themselves safe up until now because of the inaccessibility of the terrain or where they had carried out their acts of terror undisturbed because of the lack of sufficient German troops."[23]

The Plenipotentiary Commanding General in Serbia confirmed that "the Mihailović group can be considered beaten" and reported further: "In a proclamation circulated by radio and propaganda leaflets, to the Serbian population, Mihailović was proscribed as a criminal insurgent and a price of 200,000 dinars was put on his head. Many Mihailović supporters have apparently fled into the woods and mountains. Reports are at hand according to which Mihailović supporters who are now without a leader, try to transfer to the Četnik units of Kosta Pećanac, or to lose themselves among the Serbian Gendarmerie. Signs are also present which indicate that certain Serbian government circles tried to contact Mihailović at the last moment in order to spare Serbian blood. In the same order were the efforts of Minister President Nedić which were directed at preventing a too severe action against the Mihailović supporters which were allegedly forced to give battle. Investigations have shown that a member of the government, Minister of the Interior Aćimović tried in conversations to contact Mihailović through Colonel Mušicki of the Serbian Auxiliary Gendarmerie. Two Serbian Gendarmerie officers commissioned for this task were seized by German troops. A court martial action has been instituted against Mušicki as well as against the other Gendarmerie and Četnik officers who were implicated."

Communist partisan activity had also diminished, General of Artillery Bader further reported: "Thanks doubtless, to the Serbian Gendarmerie and also partly to the Četnik units which are loyal to the government and have recently fought well against them. Because of this there will be scarcely any major operations on the part of the insurgents in Serbia in the coming winter months. Band activity will be restricted in general to acts of terror and sabotage." General of Artillery Bader continued: "In spite of this however the Serbian insurgent movement cannot be considered as finally suppressed. The relative pacification which has now set in must not delude us into thinking that it is only a question of temporary condition. Doubtless the greatest danger lies in the fact that a large quantity of rifles and ammunition is still in the possession of the Serbs—in the hands of numerous illegal and so-called legal organizations. With the arrival of warmer weather the insurgent movement will flare up again, especially if the overall situation should require a withdrawal of large troop units from Serbia." Therefore General of Artillery Bader considered as his most important task during the coming months the final pacification of Serbia and the prevention of a resurgence of the insurgent movement. This was to be attained by sufficient safeguarding of the transport lanes of the industrial centers, a large scale, well prepared disarming action, the seizure and deportation of active Serbian officers, a speedy activation of German and Serbian administrations in the territories re-occupied by the unit, a reorganization of the Serbian police forces, a continuous, adequate propagandist influencing of the Serbian population.

The group of nationalist insurgents seemed to be beaten. In December the Mihailović supporters no longer gave battle in the Serbian area. About the middle of the month only dispersed remnants of Mihailović units tried to re-assemble twice in the region of Užice, but withdrew before our troops to the Drina and into the Bosnian insurgent territory.

The formation of communist bands was reported around Krupanje and in the territory between Valjevo and Požega. These bands too withdrew before our troops (342nd and 113th Infantry Divisions and units of the 717th Infantry Division) on to Croatian territory.

The remainder of the bands which had been forced back south of the Morava valley, had re-assembled south of Ivanjica and in Montenegrin-Serbian territory west of Novi Pazar. The sparse Italian garrison was apparently not in a position to advance against them.

Further band remnants had apparently reinforced the insurgents in the region of Lebane and Leskovac. In this region the influence of Kosta Pecanac seemed to be on the wane. In the middle of December, a band, 1,000 men strong, was reported near Lebane later confirmed by our air reconnaissance. Units of the 717th Infantry Division were committed. The operation near Lebane however brought no clarification, for the majority of these bands were able to escape to the south, another group over the Serbian-Bulgarian frontier and an additional one into the region of Prokuplje-Kuršumlije.

In addition to these individual local flare-ups of the insurgent movement, sabotage acts continued, especially in the district around Niš. Small bands appeared again around December 20 in the vicinity of the Danube between Vk. Gradiste and Kladova. They were broken up by units of the 704th Infantry Division. Around this time bandit activity flared up again locally around Krupanje and Valjevo. Units of the 342nd Infantry Division were committed again for small mopping up operations. During the last days of December scattered partisan groups were reported in the region of Šabac near Gr. Mitrovica, near Ub, east of Višegrad and south of Užice in the Zlatibor mountains.

Losses in the period from December 6-25, 1941:

Own: 8 dead, 10 wounded,

Russian factory guard: 3 dead, 1 wounded,

Insurgents: 763 dead (of whom 409 were shot in reprisal)

         715 prisoners

The number of hostages shot from the beginning of the insurgent movement until 12.5.1941 was given as 11,164, the number shot in camps as 558.

IV

THE FLARING UP OF THE BAND WAR IN BOSNIA

AUGUST UNTIL DECEMBER 1941

1. Internal tension in Croatia

The internal situation of the new Croatian State, which had come into being as a result of the collapse of Yugoslavia at Easter 1941, became increasingly difficult soon after it was founded. The reason for this was that the Croats wanted to rule their young country according to the principle of a unified national state. Among influential persons in Zagreb it was acknowledged that the new Croatia was not a national state, but rather a state of many nationalities. The most difficult problem was presented by the two million Serbs who were settled in restricted Serbian settlements. The Croatian State was not able to find a tenable relationship with its national minorities. There were indeed influential men in the Croatian government, with the Poglavnik* at the head, who seriously tried to master the difficulties by trying to set up the new state "on the model of the Dolfuss-Schuschnigg Austrian State!" The Pravoslav (Serbian Orthodox) section of the people were also to have equal rights, but it was doubtful whether the "representative would rather enter the framework of a professional state any more than the National Socialists did in a dying Austria."[1]

In addition to the national differences there was the religious intolerance of the Catholic Croats towards the Orthodox and the Moslems living in Bosnia. Apart from all these difficulties, the expulsion of the Serbs by the Ustasha units was the main reason for the insurgent movement which flared up throughout the whole country. "The sacrifice of the blood of its citizens, which the Croatian State had demanded since its inception, surpassed by far that of Yugoslavia during its entire existence," the German General in Zagreb reported. "The aversion against the Ustasha movement felt by everyone who did not directly profit by it was widespread. The capital 'U' in the Croatian insignia had become the symbol of the "Gessler" hat for a broad strata of the Croatian nation." There was continued news of Ustasha misdeeds, excesses of murder and robbery, which led to an increase in the insurgent movement in the territories populated by Croats.

---

* "Leader" of the Independent State of Croatia, Ante Pavelić, head of the Croatian Ustasha organization.

2. Combatting of Insurgency
August to October 1941

Until the beginning of August, major disturbances by armed bands were only reported in the region southwest of Banja Luka. Small centers of unrest however were discernable near Prijedor, Bos. Kastajnice, Bos. Brod, Doboj, Naglaj, northeast of Valjevo, near Mokro and Sokalac. Sabotage acts were also directed against the railroad through Banja Luka-Prijedor-Bos. Brod-Sarajevo and Doboj-Tuzla. Until now only one surprise attack had taken place against German Wehrmacht installations. At the beginning the Croatian Wehrmacht successfully combatted the local unrest. If the unrest in Serbia spread to Croatia and developed contrary to the interests of the German Wehrmacht, then a sharp intervention by the German troops, admittedly small in number, in Croatia, would occur.

From approximately the beginning of August the bands in Bosnia appeared in greater numbers. In addition local centers of unrest existed too. Surprise attacks were met with the severest counter measures. Apparently band activity from Serbia now spread to Bosnia, especially the region northeast of Sarajevo.

However, the Croats still remained masters of the situation, and the continually changing unrest which flared up was suppressed by the commitment of German and Croatian troops in small, local mopping up operations. In the middle of August the insurgents were thrown back near Kostajica, by the cooperation of our troops and air forces. The Croats mopped up the area south of Prijedor (Bos. Krupa-Bihac-Bos. Petrovac). By the end of August the movement of bands which had been forced out of Serbia into Bosnia had been confirmed. They attempted to cross the Drina between Bijeljina and Zvornik.

In September the activity of the bands continued to grow. About the middle of the month our national defense battalions met with strong resistance during an engagement with insurgents in the vicinity of Doboj. Attacks continued to be directed against the Bihaj-Tuzla-and-Doboj-Sarajevo railroad. Our troops had scarcely cleaned up the situation in Doboj and restored the interrupted railroads when new insurgent groups were reported west of Zvornik and on the Tuzla-Doboj road.

Towards the end of the month new concentrations of bands in connection with the insurgent movement in Serbia operated west of the Drina with the main point of attack around Zvornik. Here the insurgents had committed mortars and heavy machine guns. Bands also appeared in the area of Bijeljina.

Attempts by the insurgents to cross the Drina were repulsed. A rather strong band movement prevailed in the area northeast and east of Sarajevo in the Javor and Romanja mountains. It was scarcely possible to maintain traffic on the Sarajevo-Zvornik road and the garrison of Zvornik was encircled by the insurgents.

Advance of the Italians up to the demarcation line

At the beginning of October weak Italian units advanced into the upper Drina valley towards Foča and Goražde. On October 9 strong units of the Italian Second Army (General Ambrosio) advanced from the "demilitarized zone" as far as the German-Italian demarcation line, to the line of Karlova-Topuska-Sanski-Marcal Vakuf-D. Vakuf-Bugojno-Vakuf grn.-Prozor-Kalinovok-Gorazde.

On this situation the German General in Zagreb reported to the Wehrmacht Commander Southeast that he feared that the Četniks, instead of being encircled and captured by the advancing Italians, would be forced on to the territory of the German zone, only to re-inforce the Četniks already there, and would endanger more than ever the Banja Luka-Prijedor railroad towards Sarajevo. According to credible reports several Četnik leaders had gone from Montenegro to Albania, where they had been received with joy by the population. They were purportedly there to prepare a large scale revolt against the Italians in the coming Spring.[2]

At the beginning of October the insurgents in East Bosnia received strong support from Serbia and attacked Zvornik. Several Croatian battalions were brought up from Tuzla for the relief of Zvornik. On the 8th Zvornik was freed from the insurgents. A few days later however the insurgents made a renewed thrust against the Tuzla-Zvornik road. In the mountains southwest of Zvornik there were rather large sized bands which were estimated at 6,000 men and which received continual reinforcements across the Drina from Serbia. The battles before Zvornik continued. Artillery was used by both sides. The Croatians could not drive off the insurgents west of Zvornik before the 19th of October, when they retreated towards the west into the mountains.

Lack of German troops

In the meantime three local defense battalions had been trans-ported to Croatia at the beginning of October: Battalion 447 went to Sarajevo, the 925th to Zagreb and the 823rd to Banja Luka. These three battalions as well as the two local defense battalions in Susak and Doboj, the 923rd and the 924th had to act as support for railroad security. After the arrival of the three new battalions the German

General in Zagreb originally intended to commit the 718th Infantry Division mainly to secure the extensive Drina railroad from Bijeljina to Višegrad to prevent a return to Bosnia of the bands which had been driven out of Serbia. Other units of the division were to be used for combatting the insurgents in northwest Serbia. The previously mopped up assembly area of the bands in Eastern Bosnia, the Romanja and Javor mountains had to be given up as sufficient troops were not available.[3] The insurgents also remained active in the areas of Banja Luka, around Sarajevo, and on the Bos. Brod-Doboj-Tuzla railroad. Therefore all troops of the 718th Infantry Division which were still available had to be committed for the mopping up of these insurgent centers.

In the meantime, however, the Croatian garrisons of Višegrad and Rogatica in south Bosnia were encircled by the insurgents. Here too the besiegers received fresh support from Serbia. On October 21 Rogatica fell to the insurgents.

On the same day the German General in Zagreb reported on this matter to the Wehrmacht Commander Southeast:

"The fighting capacity of the Croatian troops is diminishing so much that they can no longer hold their own against the insurgents. The 718th Infantry Division is too weak to help them. If the Croats should have to request help from the Italians for the garrison encircled in Visegrad, because help cannot be given from the German side, we shall not have the moral right to prevent this in spite of the loss of prestige to the German Wehrmacht. Therefore the German General in Zagreb urgently requests that the dispatch of a division, released from the Eastern front to the Serbian area, be effected."

The Wehrmacht Commander Southeast however could not make available the reinforcements requested for Croatia for the present. He informed the German General in Zagreb on October 22 that the transport of at least two divisions to Serbia was urgent. Should a further division be available later its transfer to Croatia would be recommended. The OKH agreed to this interpretation.

On the same day the Wehrmacht Commander Southeast, in a telegram to Belgrade, declared himself in agreement with the intention of the Plenipotentiary Commanding General in Serbia to withdraw the 718th Infantry Division to Serbia. In spite of everything the Plenipotentiary Commanding General in Serbia transferred units of this division into the Drina-Sava bend in order to relieve the 342nd Infantry Division there, for a joint attack on Užice in cooperation with the newly arrived 113rd Infantry Division.

The Croatian Wehrmacht

Here it might be expedient to make a few remarks about the Croatian Wehrmacht.

At the end of 1941 the young Croatian Wehrmacht comprised about 46 battalions. Six divisions were concentrated in three corps units. In addition there were about 15 Ustasha battalions, with one mountain battery, the bodyguard of the Poglavnik (one motorized regiment and one cavalry troop) and four additional specialized battalions (railroad security and Volksdeutsche operational echelons).

Germany had supplied practically all its armament from its captured enemy material stocks. Delivery by the Italians was below standard. The clothing of the Croatian Wehrmacht was rather bad. The troops fighting in Bosnia were short of good shoes, boots, overcoats, blankets, tents, winter underwear, etc. In contrast the Ustasha battalions which were composed of volunteers were far better off as to clothing, equipment and pay, than the Croatian Wehrmacht soldiers. The morale of the Croatian army units at the front also suffered because of this lack of equipment. Signs of disintegration had already appeared in some of the units.

Concerning the constitution of the young Croatian Wehrmacht, General von Glaise Horstenau wrote: "It is part of the tragedy of this young state which is scarcely able to function in its present hybrid composition, that it was not allowed to create more than a militia of the most modest pretensions from the excellent military material, which had won fame for centuries on the battlefields of Europe. With little or no training and some hardly adequate Yugoslav experience, the units were opposed months ago to a clever and resolute enemy. They marched and fought, only seldom relieved, in the Bosnian mountains, and were now very tired. Certainly a few units have fought with distinction, such as the few companies which held Visegrad for 70 days. But in general the attack and resistance capacity of the Croatian soldier fell from week to week. Offensive operations remained static as a rule after the first attack, defensive battles ended in panic. Military discipline also left much to be desired. Insubordination, mutiny, and desertion increased. All this reflected weariness and lack of training, but also the refusal to engage in a struggle regarded, in wide circles of the Croatian people, as a civil war, whose outbreak and expansion was blamed on the fury of the hated Ustasha. General Glaise described the Officer and NCO Corps as too old, or spoiled by their Yugoslav service. Among the officers differences

between the former Austrian and the former Yugoslav officers intensified and in the latter the Great Serbian-Yugoslav idea was not dead.
In addition there was also the contrast between the Ustasha favored
by Marshal Kvaternik and the Croatian Wehrmacht.

Aggravation of the situation

At the beginning of December, at the time of the advance of the
342nd and 113th Infantry Divisions on Užice, an increasing unrest
was noticeable in the previous centers of the revolt—Sarajevo-Doboj-
Tuzla, due to the influx of numerous dispersed bands which had
been driven out of Serbia. Now however the unrest also filtered into
the northwestern part of the German occupied area of Croatia. Skir-
mishes and surprise attacks increased once more in the whole Bosnian area between the Sava and the demarcation line.

An operation which was launched in the middle of December
south and southeast of Doboj in the Ozren Mountains was only partially successful with the mopping up by the Croats of the heights
east of the Doboj-Naglaj line. The insurgent movement ventured
more and more against the industries important to the war economy
situated north and northeast of Sarajevo. There had already been destruction of the electric power cables.

The fighting qualities of the Croatian troops were no longer sufficient to quell the revolt in Bosnia. To be sure the measures of the
Italian occupation troops influenced in part the defensive combat of
the Croats. If such developments continued, revolts of a large and
dangerous extent would have to be reckoned with. Here a word concerning the relation of the Croats to our allies the Italians. General
Glaise reported in detail on this subject on November 21 to the Wehrmacht Commander Southeast:

"Naturally it is the duty of the German representative unhindered
by considerations of popularity, to shore up as much as possible this
poorly supported (Croatian) government. In this, to be sure, we
place ourselves in silent opposition to our Italian allies who show no
interest in strengthening the situation of the Croatian regime which
because of its friendliness to Germany, is not particularly acceptable
to the Italians. The episode of the Croatian garrison of Višegrad is
only one example of many. Although Rome and Zagreb had agreed
that this really brave unit should remain at rest for a temporary re-
cuperation, the local Italian military forces had demanded their immediate withdrawal. In a very friendly conversation, Oxilia (representative of the Italian Wehrmacht in Zagreb) informed me only

today that the Croats from Višegrad who had been merely transferred for their own rehabilitation to Goražde, were speedily returned to Višegrad after only a few days."

General Glaise then continued: "The whole area south of the demarcation line had been completely transferred to the Italians. In Bihać and Mostar one could see Italian commanders and Cetnik leaders walking around the main square peaceably. Insurgents coming from the mountains even effected their purchases with the help of Italian soldiers and then returned unmolested to their woods. The animosity of the Italian military authorities to the government even expressed itself in a sympathetic gesture to the local Croats by paralyzing the Ustasha. To be sure the Četniks also showed their gratitude by giving the Italians a free hand. There were practically no fights between Italians and Cetniks."

And in another report on the situation in the middle of December, General Glaise made the following report: "The Italian question has retained in the Croatian area the aspect it has held up until now. Strong efforts at expansion, decisive opposition towards Croatian independence, and the greatest jealousy of every German influence what so ever. It was a policy of patience and toleration as far as the Panslavs (i.e., the Orthodox population) and the insurgent movement was concerned, in the opinion expressed by the Croatian State leader to General Oxilia, despite strong criticism." The insurgents, estimated at 2,500 men, were able to withdraw undisturbed from Višegrad according to agreement, in the direction of Sarajevo. General Glaise continued: "Such methods couold indicate that the Italian troops which at the moment numbered nine divisions (in the area south of the demarcation line), would allow the insurgents time and rest during the wintertime, to prepare themselves undisturbed for the coming Spring."

"The attitude of the Italian occupation troops has been definitely pro-Serb until now."

To be sure General Glaise also brought to the attention of the Wehrmacht Commander Southeast, that in certain Croatian circles, which were disappointed by the German Reich's lack of interest in the Croatian question, the opinion was expressed, that a complete surrender of all Croatia to the Italians would be preferable to the present situation. Even the Poglavnik, whose friendship towards Germany no one doubted, had expressed the opinion that Croatia would be much better off it it would depend less on Mussolini than on his political opponents.[4]

Estimate of the situation

Around the middle of December the German General in Zagreb estimated that "the insurgent movement in the Croatian area northeast of the demarcation line had, in spite of the rather mild winter, increased rather than decreased as far as territory was concerned. It covered now nearly all of Northern Bosnia and also the "Kordun," the former Austrian military frontier territory southeast of Zagreb, but even branched out into the Sava valley towards Slavonia and Syrmia. The leading idea of the partisan struggle is still a mixture between a vague Communism and Panslavism. In addition to the Croatian Communists the Moslems have also joined the Panslav insurgents![5]

Colonel Mihailović, who had fled from Serbia, took over command of the fight in East Bosnia in December. Croatian reports state that the Četnik leader Dangić, who was operating in the Romanja mountains, was not willing to subordinate himself to Mihailović. In three places the insurgents had entered into negotiations. Delegates of the insurgents who had negotiated with Croatian officers in the vicinity of Sarajevo declared: "We will never lay down our arms before the end of the war, for we are fighting against Fascism and the oppressors of the Slavs. We have no fight with the Croatian people and the Croatian Wehrmacht, we are only enemies of the Ustasha. Russia will be victorious!" Other reports stated that Dangić did not want to fight against the German Wehrmacht, but only wanted to protect the Panslavs (i.e., the Orthodox population) from the outrages of the Ustasha against the Communists in East Bosnia.

It was indicative of the confused relations when Marshal Kvaternik, obviously excited, said during a conversation with the German General in Zagreb, he had learned from various sources that Nedic, the Serbian Prime Minister, was in collusion with the "commander of the Yugoslav army," General Mihailović, in order to conduct the revolt with him either in the Spring or at a later opportunity. On the other hand the Serbian Minister for Home Affairs, Acimovic, had disseminated the rumor that Germany sooner or later wanted to bring to power an independent Serbia, which was to consist of present day Old Serbia, as far as Skoplje, of the Banat, East Syrmia and East Bosnia as far as the Drina. Moreover, Nedić, Mihailović and the Italians agreed to transfer the revolt to Croatia and thereby to demonstrate that the young Croatian State was incapable of holding its ground.

The German troops committed in Croatia (718th Infantry Division and five regional defense battalions) were drawn more and more during the recent months into the civil war in a country which was to be united with Italy with the Duke of Spoleto designated as King. Understandably, the German General in Zagreb, in this discordant and ambiguous situation, remarked that "it was a pity that every drop of German blood that flowed was spilled in a land which was tied to an allied power and which had so many free troops at its disposal." To be sure German troops only interfered where the interest of the German war economy or the safety of our own troops was at stake.

Our troops therefore laid the main stress on the protection of the Zagreb-Belgrade-Bos. Brod-Sarajevo railroad which was in a parlous condition. The Zagreb-Belgrade railroad more and more became the scene of sabotage acts. The secondary Sisak-Prijedor railroad, which led to the Lublja mines and the most important railroad, the Brod-Sarajevo line, passed directly through insurgent territory. The German war economy also had a particular interest in the Sarajevo-Tuzla-Zenica area. "From this picture it follows," General Glaise estimated, "that German military interest in Croatia, with the exception of the main Zagreb-Belgrade railroad, is extending towards East Bosnia, where the revolt situation is most critical, and therefore to Sarajevo." He proposed to the Plenpotentiary Commanding General in Serbia that battalions of the 718th Infantry Division be withdrawn from Zagreb and Banja Luka and so create an opportunity for this division to concentrate in the area of Sarajevo-Doboj-Tuzla. The Plenipotentiary Command General in Serbia agreed to this proposal.

Towards the end of December, the 718th Infantry Division moved against the insurgent territory in southeast Bosnia. Parts of the division reached Tuzla from the northeast and east, and Doboj, Zavidovici and Vareš from the north. The situation in Bosnia had developed in this fashion in December, when in the middle of the month a new directive of the OKW arrived which occasioned surprise to the Wehrmacht Commander Southeast, and the greatest confusion among Croatian military leaders.

New directives of the OKW

The change in the situation in Russia at the end of 1941 had made it necessary to throw all available troops to the Eastern front. Therefore the OKW directed the Wehrmacht Commander Southeast on December 16 to free forces in Serbia and Croatia for the German army in the east, starting with the reinforcements which had been assigned to him only a few weeks previously, the 113th and 342nd Infantry Divisions. Bulgarian, Italian, and in case of need even

Rumanian and Hungarian troops were to be moved into Serbia and Croatia to take over the task of re-establishing peace and order in place of the German occupation troops.[7]

The Italian High Command, to whom the German General in Rome conveyed this request, declared its readiness to allow troops of the Italian 2nd Army to move into Croatia, in order to relieve the German troops stationed east of the demarcation line, as soon as the necessary agreement was reached with the Croatian government.[8]

These intentions did not appear objectionable. However, on December 16 the Chief of Staff of the German General in Zagreb Lt. Colonel v. Funk, telegraphed to the Wehrmacht Commander Southeast:

"The Italian 2nd Army could scarcely guarantee the suppression of the revolt in Bosnia. It is occupied with the strong unrest in Gatta, Foča, and along the Split-Karlstadt railroad. The Italian methods up until now have fanned rather than suppressed the revolt. If the Italian 2nd Army were to be responsible for the whole of Croatia, a spreading of the revolt is to be feared among the Croatian population. It appears necessary to leave the German division (718th) in Croatia, in order to maintain the security area and thereby the demarcation line, and to let the German power in this area remain independent of the Italian 2nd Army. I would prefer this situation to the obvious extremely serious political and economic consequences which would accompany an occupation of Croatia by the Italian 2nd Army."[9]

Suggestions of the Wehrmacht Commander Southeast

The Wehrmacht Commander Southeast also considered as a prerequisite for the deployment of Italians in Croatia and Bulgarians in Serbia, that sufficient German forces be left in these two countries to maintain the security of the industrial areas essential to the war. In addition, one command of the entire Serbian area, and control of the Military Administration, the Serbian civil administration including the Serbian police and the transportation system in Serbia and Croatia must remain in German hands. The German General in Zagreb was also to remain. The possibility of a deployment of Hungarian and Rumanian troops was to be given up. The Wehrmacht Commander Southeast reported this to the OKW on December 20 and proposed at the same time that "the Plenipotentiary Commanding General retains control in Serbia over the military administration as well as the subordinate Bulgarian units, and at the same time he conducts the task of the Commander in Serbia.

"The Italian 2nd Army retains the high command in Croatia. The plants in Sarajevo, Jajce and Prijedor remain in German hands to safeguard the areas important for the German war economy.

"In Serbia the following are to be secured by German units: the capital, Belgrade; Bor (copper); the territory around Krupanje-Bosnica (antimony, lead, tin); Ivanjica (antimony) and Prijedor (iron).

"The Bulgarian units take over the security of southeast Serbia from the Old Serbian frontier to a line running from Priština via Mitrovica, then east of the Ibar valley via Trstenik to Kragujevac, Lapova and further east via Zlot as far as Rogatina.

"The Italian 2nd Army occupies the whole of Croatia with the exception of the area around Sarajevo, Jajce and Prijedor. Of special importance is the absolute protection of the Belgrade-Zagreb and Brod-Sarajevo railroad which is vital to German units in Croatia are to be subordinated tactically to the Italian 2nd Army but to be left as now in the area of Sarajevo, Jajce and Prijedor.

"For these tasks the following *German forces* are necessary in Serbia: 2 divisions each of 3 regiments, or 3 divisions each of 2 regiments (704th, 714th, and 717th Infantry Divisions), in addition 3 regional defense battalions which were in Serbia up until now, army units and 3 regional defense battalions to be brought in from Croatia.

"In Croatia. 1 division consisting of 2 regiments (718th Infantry Division) and the two regional defense battalions which have been in Croatia up until now, under a unified command.

"Bulgarian forces in Serbia: three divisions.

"Italian forces in Croatia: according to the estimate there, 6 divisions.

"The displacements in Serbia are dependent on the entry of the Bulgarian forces. The entry of Italian forces into Croatia can take place as quickly as possible. The withdrawal of the 113th Infantry Division and then of the 342nd Infantry Division can only take place after the relief of the 704th, 714th and 717th divisions by Bulgarian forces. Probable time for the evacuation of the 113th Infantry Division, the end of January, for the 342nd Infantry Division, the beginning of February 1942. A previous withdrawal of these two divisions would not be tenable, since otherwise setbacks and a considerable destruction of localities could not be prevented.

"Should this commitment of forces appear altogether too high, the handing over of the whole Croatian territory to the Italians is recommended, because the German forces in Serbia are more important."[10]

On December 22 General Glaise reported the confusion which the German intentions had produced among the leading military personalities: Marshal Kvaternik and General Laxa were "disconcerted" in the face of the new situation. They feared the most difficult internal developments and a threat to the whole Balkans. Marshal Kvaternik had requested that the 718th Infantry Division be left in Croatia and had declared himself ready to build up the Croatian Legion in Russia to the strength of a complete division. He had also requested that a mopping up operation might be carried out in East Bosnia at the beginning of the coming year under German leadership, with the 718th Infantry Division, three to six German battalions from Serbia, and Croatian units, as well as with Italian units, from Višegrad in case of need.

General Glaise offered the following suggestion to the Wehrmacht Commander Southeast with regard to the new directive of the OKW:

The 718th Infantry Division was to remain with one group of regiments around Sarajevo, and with another around Tuzla, since the industrial installation vital to Germany in this territory had to be protected and the insurgents had received strong reinforcements in Serbia because of our offensive operations. One of the two regional defense battalions was to be transferred to Prijedor, but the protection of the Jajce works could be left to the Italians.

The German General in Zagreb and the German ambassador considered it important to leave one regional defense battalion in Zagreb because of German interest in Croatia. Major General Glaise stated that the German ambassador would be extremely grateful if the Brod-Belgrade railroad section remained under German protection and thereby assured a certain German influence opposed the zealous interference of the Italians in the fertile region of Syrmia, which was populated by numerous Volkdeutsche, and was essential for the provisioning of Semlin and Belgrade. The remaining railroad security could be left to the Italians, even the Bosna Valley railroad, and that of eastern Bosnia, Sarajevo-Rogatica-Višegrad. Sarajevo could be considered as a garrison for the 718th Infantry Division, and to be sure, must also house an Italian garrison. The Commander of the 718th Infantry Division should be made the garrison commander of Sarajevo. Otherwise it would be preferable to transfer the division headquarters to Tuzla. For political reasons the German ambassador in Zagreb declared himself in favor of the retention of the office of the "German General in Zagreb."[11]

In another interesting report of December 24 General Glaise described once more the deep and lasting impression which the new directives of the OKW had made on the Croatian High Command. "I foresee a great danger in the spring in a too extensive release of Serbian and Croatian territory to the Bulgarians and the Italians. Contrary to all custom the Italians had not informed the Croatian army command of their new task of moving into Croatia to establish peace and order. This forebodes no good! Furthermore the change in the German High Command by the Fuehrer caused some hesitation among the Croats."

At the same time General Glaise also depicted the vacillation of the Croatian government as a consequence of Italian influence. On December 16 he reported that the Minister of State Dr. Ante Pavelic accompanied by three ministers, one of whom was the foreign minister, the Italian ambassador and a committee of economic experts had gone to Venice, "ostensibly for economic negotiations." The actual reason however for the journey of the Poglavnik was to pay a visit to the Duke of Spoleto in Florence. The Croats expected the Italians to demand the immediate appointment of the Duke of Spoleto as King of Croatia with which they would comply.

The Commander of the Italian 2nd Army, General Ambrosio, also took part in the conversations in Venice.[12]

When the German ambassador in Zagreb informed the Poglavnik on the latter's return from Venice, of the new situation, the leader of the Croatian state was "very indignant." A certain approach towards Italian policy had been taken by the Poglavnik some weeks ago. The discussions in Venice and Florence had taken place in a very friendly spirit. Count Ciano informed the Croatian Foreign Minister in Venice: "It is better that the new King arrives a few days too late than a few days too soon." This delay was characteristic of Italian policy.

"The strengthened appearance of the Italian Wehrmacht," General Glaise judged, "will cause more difficulties for the government in Zagreb, considering the avarice which is characteristic of our allies which will affect our economic interests in the country."[13]

Resolve to suppress the revolt in Bosnia

In the meantime the Fuehrer rejected an entry of Italian troops into the German occupation zone of Croatia. In a December 24 directive of the OKW, the Wehrmacht Commander Southeast was ordered to suppress the revolt in southeast Croatia with forces of the Plenipotentiary Commanding General in Serbia in collaboration with

with Croatian units and with the commitment of the 342nd Infantry Division which would be available until the end of January. The collaboration of Italian units was considered and was to be agreed upon with the Italian allies. The assignment of new German forces was not to be reckoned with. At the beginning of January the 113th Infantry Division had to move to the Eastern front.

At the same time the Fuehrer had commissioned the Wehrmacht Commander Southeast to request the Royal Bulgarian War Ministry to move Bulgarian troops into southeastern Serbia in order to maintain peace and order in the territory proposed by the Wehrmacht Commander Southeast. This was to be agreed upon as quickly as possible with the Bulgarians.

On December 24 the Wehrmacht Commander Southeast applied to the Bulgarian War Ministry through the Bulgarian liaison officer, General Zilkoff, with the request that approximately three Bulgarian divisions under a unified command be subordinated tactically to the Plenipotentiary Commanding General in Serbia. The rapid transfer of these Bulgarian fighting forces into the Old Serbian territory was requested, in order to free the German forces there (342nd Infantry Division) for the combatting of the revolt in Croatia and for another commitment (113th Infantry Division). The German forces (717th Infantry Division) situated in Leskovac, Kruševac, Cuprije, Jagodina, Aleksinac and Zaječar was to be relieved immediately by January 15 by the Bulgarian units and the occupation of the whole area was to be completed on January 15.[14]

At the same time the Plenpotentiary Commanding General in Serbia was ordered, following the entry of the Bulgarian troops, to free the 113th and the 342nd Infantry Divisions, the 113rd for transport to the Eastern front beginning on January 1, and the 342nd for commitment in Croatia. The most important units of the 113rd Infantry Division were to be relieved with the first troops of the 717th Infantry Division which had been made available by the Bulgarians, so that they might be ready for evacuation on January 1. With the further entry of Bulgarian units the 717th Infantry Division gradually took over the security tasks in the area occupied up until now by the 113th Infantry Division. By changes in the position of the units of the 704th and 714th Infantry Divisions, the 342nd Infantry Division was to be made available in its occupation zone, so that it was assembled from the middle of January on the western boundary of its present zone, for the suppression of the revolt in southeast Croatia. From February on the 342nd Infantry Division must likewise be available for transport to the Eastern front.

V

COMBATTING THE REVOLT IN BOSNIA
JANUARY TO MARCH 1942

1. Mopping up operations in the area Višegrad-Zvornik

Situation at the beginning of 1942

As in the last months of the previous year the insurgents continued to develop their activity according to plan at the beginning of 1942 in the areas of Bijelina-Tuzla-Doboj-Sarajevo. In the Italian zone of occupation centers of unrest existed especially in the area south of Sarajevo and south of Višegrad. The influx of insurgents from Old Serbia into East Bosnia continued. The Italians did not proceed energetically against the insurgent movement in Herzegovina, Montenegro and Dalmatia. In order to avoid the sacrifice of blood they negotiated in many places with the insurgents, even had friendly contacts with them, made use of them against the Ustasha, supported them and incited the national Serbian Četniks to fight against the Croats. Thus, a great tension existed between the Croatian government and the Italians. Croatian troops were unable to pacify their country. Only if they fought together with German troops were they of use, glad to fight and capable of being committed. Among individual Croatian units, fresh signs of disintegration appeared, and the Croats complained of the unfavourable influence of the Italians on their own troops.[1]

Preparations for the operations in East Bosnia

Mopping up action in the Ozren mountains

At the appointed time on January 15 the operation commenced, placing extraordinary demands on the troops. The insurgents had to be tracked down and brought to battle in violently cold weather, with temperatures falling to 20 and 30 degrees below, with fog and icy winds, on mountain tracks deep in snow, in a wintry, mountainous country.

The two operational divisions fell in from the east over the Drina and the west, from Sarajevo and Tuzla to take the insurgents in a pincer movement and to destroy them. Accompanied by Croatian units the 697th Infantry Regiment advanced from the Zvornik bridgehead and broke the resistance of the insurgents on the heights southwest of the town and south of it on the Drina valley road. Road blocks and destroyed bridges had to be circumvented. On the 16th the regiment pursued the retreating enemy, and after a hard fight took several of the villages defended by the insurgents and mopped up the Drinjac valley of dispersed band remnants. On the 17th the regiment advanced further south into the wintry mountain terrain of the Javor mountains, reached Vlasenica on the 18th and made contact here with the 699th Infantry Regiment.

During this period (15-18 January) the 699th Infantry Regiment advanced up along the Drina into the area west of Ljubovija, despite road blocks. Here, in the area of Milici about 400 prisoners—mostly Dangic-Četniks—were brought in, one tank, two machine guns, about 160 rifles and a considerable amount of ammunition were captured. The regiment mopped up the area from the west as far as Vlasenica. One battalion reached Srebrenica on the 13th without meeting any enemy.

Stretching far beyond Užice to seal off the insurgent territory from the south, the 698th Infantry Regiment was committed against Višegrad instead of the dilatory Italians. Part of the regiment advanced on the 15th from Višegrad through the upper Drina valley to Mededa. Later the Italians blockaded this area. Other parts of the 698th Infantry Regiment in the meantime fought their way through from Višegrad to the west and reached Rogatica on the 17th. An Italian alpine battalion joined the advance of the German column and followed it as far as Rogatica on the 20th. In addition to this one Italian and two "Black Shirt" battalions took part in the operation by putting on a "demonstration" in Foča. The Ravenna Division which was intended to block off the south did not arrive, allegedly because of the destruction of the railroad near Mostar. Its movement would be delayed a few weeks longer.

In the following days (January 18-21) the 342nd Infantry Division mopped up the area which they had entered. The 698th Infantry Regiment combed the region of Rogatica, where about 50 insurgents fell in battle, 200 prisoners were taken, and 63 captured Croats were freed. The 699th Infantry Regiment patrolled the area of Ljubovija as far as Vlasenica and Srebrenica. Meanwhile the 697th Infantry Regiment advanced from Vlasenica through the Javor Mountains further southwards, met only weak enemy resistance and occupied Pijesak without a fight on January 22. Elements of the regiment advanced on the 22nd from Han Pijesak westwards to Olovo. This strenuous mopping up operation ended without any important results. For the most part the insurgents had escaped in time the encirclement which threatened them.

The 718th Infantry Division too was only able to seize elements of the insurgents who had been forced into this pocket. The 738th Infantry Regiment started from Sarajevo on January 15, in order to advance through the wild Romanja Mountains to Rogotica and northeastwards via Sokolac. Fighting in the most difficult terrain, the regiment made its way through the snow-covered Karst Mountains. The insurgents were driven from their rocky positions and hiding places; 240 were taken prisoner, 6 machine guns, 1 mortar, 50 mines, 160 hand grenades and 25,000 rounds of infantry ammunition were captured. In addition 10 captured Italians and 57 Croats were liberated. On the 21st the 738th Infantry Regiment took Padromanija in spite of weak enemy resistance. On the 22nd elements of the regiment pressed beyond Sokolac which two days previously had been bombed by Croatian aircraft, to Han Pijesak via Prača towards Rogatica.

The 750th Infantry Regiment which advanced with the Croats towards the south, was held up more by the difficulties of the winter and terrain than by enemy resistance. On the 16th the regiment reached Kladanje. In the following days the regiment mopped up both sides of the Stupani-Kladani highway and then advanced further through impenetrable mountains. Olivo which had been bombed by Croatian aircraft was reached on the 22nd. The enemy had retreated from here too. On the 23rd the regiment made contact with Croatian battalions, which in the meantime had warded off attempts of the insurgents to break through.

On January 23, through an unhappy misfortune, Vlasenica, which had been occupied by Croatian and German troops since the 18th was bombed by Italian aircraft. Twelve Italian aircraft had been assigned for the operation. They made their first flight from Mostar on January 23. Of the three aircraft which took off, two had to return because of engine trouble. The third, as reported, attacked Vlasenica, a result of bad orientation, although our troops had hung out Swastika flags and gave recognition to signs.

Results

On January 23 the operation to drive the insurgents into a pocket in the region of the wild Javor Mountains was concluded. The 342nd Infantry Division and the 718th Infantry Division suffered losses of 24 dead, 131 wounded and one missing, the Croats 50 dead and seriously wounded. In addition 297 men were rendered unfit to fight again in the numbing cold climate of the region. Insurgent losses totalled 521 dead. More than 1,400 guerrillas were taken prisoner. Four guns, one mortar, 22 machine guns, 855 rifles, 72 mines, 33 horses and beasts of burden and 600 cattle were brought in as loot by our troops. 168 Croats and 104 Italians were released from captivity.

In a letter to the Wehrmacht Commander Southeast. the Commander (Colonel Strauss) of the 698th Infantry Regiment wrote conerning the impressions he had gained during the operation in Southeast Bosnia:

> There were many surprises, miserable snowed-up mule tracks, infernal cold, always between 30 and 40 degrees. We could not take over any billets because there were no localities which sufficed and because many houses had been burned down. Irrespective of all the Scyllas and Charybdises which interfered with our winter odyssey, we accomplished it. The behavior of our troops was outstanding despite the great hardships. However the troops in the mountains should be equipped with mountain boots.
>
> The operation in mid-winter had to drive the Communists from their positions in the hills and disperse them. This was accomplished. The majoirty of the enemy however retreated into the woods and some of them had probably wandered away to the south into the Italian zone. On our arrival in the area of Vadiste a Communist band was reported nearly every day. They were the insurgents which we had driven from Užice previously. They were upset by our appearance, they spied around and withdrew, probably to assemble elsewhere. From the valley, it is quite impossible, especially at this time of the year, in knee-deep snow, to mop up these people. It is not even possible in summer, however improbable that may seem. It is an extremely broken, rocky terrain, with perpendicular rock faces, deep gorges, gigantic forests. Considering the wonderful signal system of the bands, whose spies lie in wait somewhere in the rocks, under a bush or at the edge of the forest, it is impossible to draw near without camouflage. When I was in Rogatica, it was reported to me that a unit of about 100 Communists was situated in a locality in the neighborhood. On the previous day, a patrol had been fired on from the heights above this village. I therefore ordered my battalion to surround the village at a distance at night. Before dawn penetration was made from all sides. The whole band, approximately 100 men was destroyed. However such operations are only successful at night. I needed the whole battalion to clear this village!

Even though our troops carried out their mission bravely, the planned encirclement and the complete destruction [of the enemy] in such an extensive area, between the Drina-Boana and Spreča was not achieved. As in previous fights with the bands, so in those hard winter days they accomplished praiseworthy results. In violent cold and driving snow, they marched along wretched roads, covered with ice, and along mule tracks, and had to fight a malicious enemy who could not be caught in a wild, mountainous country. The guerillas were everywhere and nowhere. It was possible to disperse them, pursue them but not to destroy them completely. They defended themselves in their positions in the rocks, and then quickly dispersed again into their villages, where they acted like "peaceful peasants" and behaved in a "friendly" manner towards our troops.

The action on the southern flank, the sealing off by Italian troops of the area to be mopped up, which was promised by General Ambrosio did not materialize, because the departure of the Ravenna Division was delayed for some weeks. Under these circumstances the Italians did not honour their promise completely and were satisfied to march behind our southernmost enveloping column as far as Rogatica and to demonstrate at Foča with Black Shirts. In view of such weak support by the Italian allies, the Wehrmacht Commander Southeast reported on January 21, even before the end of the operation, to the OKW:

"The Italian attitude toward the insurgent movement makes a lasting success of the German efforts doubtful. The inactivity of the Italians against the insurgents until now, the obvious denial of Italian help during the current operations in Croatia, and the attitude of the Croatian government towards the Ustasha movement, are responsible for the continued increase in the number of insurgents. Their retreat into the Italian occupation zone makes a quick suppression of the insurgents in Croatia impossible."

Therefore the Wehrmacht Commander Southeast considered "corresponding political influence, and the nomination of a leader who was to be made responsible for the establishing of ordered conditions in Croatia" to be necessary. "The subordination of all Italian, Croatian and German forces to be committed for the combatting of the revolt and the disarming of all persons and organizations including the Ustasha with the exception of the Croatian Wehrmacht and police are prerequisites to this."[2]

A report of the German General in Zagreb of January 26 was also indicative of the unfavourable opinion which had been gained recently by the Germans concerning Italian support. It states: "An Alpine division had arrived in Ragusa in place of the Ravenna Division which did not arrive. Its advance units reached Kalinovik (about January 21) without previously advancing into the area of Foča-Goražda as promised. About 200 Alpine troops from Višegrad took part in the mopping up operation in East Bosnia in conjunction with our advancing column there. The Italians had stipulated that they would follow our troops, but after their arrival in Rogatica, they could not be induced to deviate southwards in an independent operation."[3]

In a report requested by the OKW the Wehrmacht Commander Southeast expressed his views on January 29 concerning the operation: "As a consequence of the passiveness of the Italians the insurgents, with few exceptions, have withdrawn cleverly before our advancing troops into the Italian zone and into the mountains. They have only been temporarily broken up by the mopping up operation, and one must reckon with their continued presence and also with the fact that actions of the insurgents will begin again. This cannot be prevented by the Croatian troops who remain in the area already mopped up, since they are inferior in battle. It is to be expected that the insurgent actions will start again, since only a temporary dispersal and not destruction was achieved. The extent of the terrain, the mountainous country and the weather conditions did not permit the expectation of better results in view of the limited time, and the departure of the 342nd Infantry Division. A lasting pacification cannot be achieved without a concerted concentrated occupation. An effective operation is only possible in favourable weather. In the present operation the employment of forces is too great in relation to the success achieved."

"The following is essential for an energetic pacification action:

A unified high command over all German, Italian and Croatian troops, simultaneous actions in the whole Croatian area in order to hinder the retreat of the insurgents, a basic change in the Italian attitude and active fighting by the Italians, considerable reinforcement of the German troops in the German occupation zone, since one division (718th Infantry Division) composed of two regiments does not suffice, and no toleration of the Ustasha in the independent Croatian territory." "Only with these prerequisites"—the Wehrmacht Commander Southeast concluded—"is a final pacification in an area so important to the German war economy, and the security of the transport lanes to be established. Otherwise only a local mopping up of limited areas is possible with the troops available at that time."

In a telegram of February 1 the Chief of the General Staff of the German Wehrmacht expressed his opinion that the reports of the Wehrmacht Commander Southeast did not yet justify the hope that extensive revolts would not occur in the Spring. "The losses of the insurgents and the number of these liquidated are too small, the number of prisoners too large. Until now it has not been possible to break the backbone of the insurgents with draconic measures. For this purpose military measures do not suffice. By means of a very wide-spread spy system and brutal police measures, every concentration of the insurgents must be recognized in time and the concern of revolt must be nipped in the bud. These methods must be applied to a great extent after the appointment of the Higher SS and Police leader."* Finally the Chief of the General Staff of the Wehrmacht referred to the fact that the Wehrmacht Commander Southeast must get along with the troops remaining to him in the coming year and that it would be his task "to apply those methods which would guarantee success."[4] In spite of everything the bloody losses of the insurgents in Serbia had been considerable. In Serbia alone in the period from 9/1/41-1/15/42 they amounted to: 7,904 killed in battle; 12,196 shot as reprisal measures. At the same time "the application of a strict rule in the treatment of prisoners" was ordered according to the directives of the OKW. In combat or in combat areas captured persons were to be shot. In view of the insufficiently severe attacks against the insurgents in the previous summer, the Commanders were directed to prevent a too mild attitude as far as the troops were concerned.[5]

Negotiations with Nedic

During the operation in East Bosnia, the number of prisoners (1,400) was relatively high in comparison to the bloody losses of the insurgents. On the other hand it was apparent that the Dangić Četniks avoided combat with German troops and did not fire on them. This was for a special reason. In Belgrade, negotiations had taken place with the Dangić Četniks by the Germans in an effort to save German blood. On January 30 the Chief of the General Staff of the Commander in Serbia, Colonel Kewisch and Dangić met. The Serbian insurgent leader was prepared to subordinate himself with all his people to the German command in order to destroy the Communists in East Bosnia and to maintain order. On January 31 and February 1 further discussions took place between Dangić and the Minister President of the Serbian Government, Nedić, as well as with the Commander in Serbia, his Chief of Staff, the deputy Chief of the Military Administration, Dr. Kiessel and Ambassador Benzler. The German General in Zagreb was requested to report in Belgrade on the 2nd with an authorized representative of the Croatian government. General Glaise, the German Ambassador in Zagreb, SA-Obergruppenfuehrer Kasche, the Croatian State Secretary Vrančić and the Chief of the Operations Department, General Staff Colonel (Drago) Low arrived

---

* On the 21/1/42 the Fuehrer had ordered the appointment of a Higher SS and Police leader, who was to be subordinated directly to the Commander in Serbia.

in Belgrade around this time for the discussions. The limitation of the occupational rights of the Croats in East Bosnia and the formation of an administration in this territory under insurgent control demanded by Dangić, was refused by the Croatian representatives. The continuation of the discussions on the 3rd was withouth result. Dangić therefore declared that there was nothing left for him to do but to take up the fight against the Croats, for he felt himself duty bound to prevent a destruction by the Ustasha of the Serbian elements living in Croatia. Dangić was escorted back over the border to Zvornik on February 4.[6]

Nothwithstanding his appreciation of the effort to pacify East Bosnia without shedding German blood, the Wehrmacht Commander Southeast was not able to sanction the negotiations entered into with Dangić. On February 12 he informed the Commander in Serbia: "Major Dangić is a Serb and will remain one. He has only made the offer in order to use East Bosnia as his troop training ground, to overcome the winter months and to make preparations to gain East Bosnia for Serbia."

Agreements with Dangić would have led, if not now, then in the Spring to failure and to an increase of the Dangić forces. The main mistake had been to have negotiated at all with Dangić about the surrender of Croatian territory without having previously obtained the opinion of the Croatian government. In the future, permission must be obtained for negotiations of any kind. The combatting of the insurgent movement and the securing of industrial installations and the most important traffic lanes in Serbia and Bosnia still remained the task of the Commander in Serbia.[7]

Attitude of the Ustasha

On January 23 the 342nd Infantry Division, minus the 697th Infantry Regiment returned to its former quarters in Serbia, preparatory to its transfer to the east. The 697th Infantry Regiment and both regiments of the 718th Infantry Division were intended for a new mopping up operation. In place of the evacuating German troops, Croatian gendarmerie and Ustasha marched in as "liberators" for the pacification of the territory which had been mopped up. Traces of a cruel guerrilla war remained in the form of plundered, burnt out villages, empty of man and beast, as witness of the partisans and their accomplices. The Serbian population living in Croatia, men, women and children incapable of fighting, fled out of fear of the atrocities of the Ustasha across the Drina into Old Serbia after the departure of the German troops. Near Bos. Mitrovica alone at least 40,000 refugees, without any nourishment, with hardly any clothing or medical attention, were crowded together. Thousands froze to death in the severe winter, died of hunger or perished as a result of epidemics.[8]

The first phase of the pacification action in East Bosnia was concluded on January 31 with discussions in Zagreb between the Plenipotentiary Commanding General in Serbia, General of Artillery Bader, the German General in Zagreb, General Glaise, the German Ambassador, SA-Obergruppenfuehrer Kasche, and the Croatian leader of state Dr. Pavelić, as well as Field Marshal Kvaternik. At these discussions in Zagreb, the Croats met in a most willing manner all the German demands. At the wish of the Plenipotentiary Commanding General in Serbia, the whole area between the Drina-Sava and the demarcation line remained German operational territory, in which the Commander of the 718th Infantry Division, Brigadier General Fortner, by order of the Commander in Serbia, exercised military command. All the German and Croatian troops in this area, as well as the Ustasha units were subordinated to him. The Croatian civilian commissioner was appointed as liaison officer of the government in Zagreb, to the German Commander. By this means German influence on the Croatian civilian administration in the zone of operations was confirmed, and thereby reassured the population.

Change of command in the Italian Second Army

As already described, the operation in East Bosnia had produced the modest support of the Italians, and finally led to a change of command in the Italian Second Army. General Ambrosio was relieved as Supreme Commander of this army.* The German General in Zagreb thought that the German experience with inadequate Italian assistance would unfortunately confirm the conception of Marshal Kvaternik that the Italian Second Army had been strongly criticized and that possibly General Ambrosio had been relieved by the Duce on this account. Nevertheless, General Ambrosio departed from the Supreme Command of the Italian Second Army as the new Chief of the Italian General Staff. General Glaise considered that a strong political general was now at the head of the Italian army, whose intention was to gain mastery over the Croatian government. General Ambrosio was considered an opponent of Croatian independence. In a conversation with the Chief of the German Liaison Staff with the Italian Second Army, he advocated a division of Croatia between Italy and Germany, with the territory south of the demarcation line to come completely into the possession of the Italians.[9]

---

* He was replaced by General Roatta, former Chief of the Italian General Staff.

Memorandum on the situation in the Southeast area

In the meantime a memorandum on the situation in the South-eastern area had been prepared in the operational staff of the Twelfth Army. In it the Wehrmacht Commander Southeast set forth the following to the OKW: "The withdrawals of four complete infantry divisions (5th and 6th Mountain Divisions, 113th and 342nd Infantry Divisions) to the east, our inferiority at sea with regard to warships and transport space, the inferiority of the German air force in the Mediterranean area, as well as the extraordinary difficulties in the supply and transport situation on land and at sea, had changed the situation in the southeastern area in the autumn of 1941 more and more in favour of England. The forces of the Wehrmacht Commander Southeast, as well as his authority no longer sufficed in any case to guarantee defense of the Southeastern area."

Concerning the situation in Serbia and Croatia, "the measures taken up until now have brought about a certain pacification. It will never be possible to cut out local unrest caused by communist partisan or national Serbian allied groups, as long as Russian and English propaganda is effective. With our present forces this cannot be avoided. The most important centers of industry and the main lines of communication are secured. Cooperation with the Bulgarian occupation troops is running according to plan. The provisioning of the troops is secured. In March it is intended to release one division staff and an infantry regiment (717th Infantry Division) to reinforce the area of Salonika. A further weakening of the German troops in Serbia can however no longer be taken into account.

"In Croatia the situation had developed alarmingly by degrees. The Croatian government and the Croatian Wehrmacht were not in a position to carry through their intentions regarding construction, either internally or with regard to the Serbian minorities and the insurgents. Unrestrained encroachments by the Ustasha upon the Croatian volunteer corps, increased the unrest in the country, rather than pacifying it. The present situation in Croatia represents a grave threat in the northern Balkans, since the Serbian will to resist continually receives new impetus from the success of the insurgents against the Croats and the Italians. The possbility of the revolt spreading to the Old Serbia area endangering communications vital for the Southeast, continues to exist.

"In case of an English offensive operation but more especially of a change of front by Turkey, a further increase of unrest must be taken into account, especially in Moslem populated areas. The Italian occupation forces are also responsible for the present conditions for in no instance have they ever attacked energetically." The Wehrmacht Commander hoped for relief *"only through a concerted and simultaneous advance of all German, Italian and Croatian troops under a unified command."*

The memorandum specified that there would be "no further withdrawal of German forces from the Serbian and Croatian areas, since otherwise the active combatting of insurgents is no longer possible, and the hinterland will no longer remain firmly enough in our possession." For all these reasons, the Wehrmacht Commander Southeast proposed once more to the OKW, as he had already done on January 21 and 29:

"The creation of a unified high command in Croatia for the suppression of the revolt there."[10]

1. Continuation of the War against the Bands in Bosnia February to March 1942

After the conclusion of the mopping up operation in the Ozren mountains the 697th Infantry Regiment of the 342nd Infantry Division departed from Bosnia. The two regiments of the 718th Infantry Division returned at the beginning of February to their garrisons in Tuzla and Sarajevo. Even during these troop movements, the dispersed bands united, as was expected, in the east Bosnian mountain region patrolled by our troops, in the area between Zvornik-Sarajevo-Rogatica-Olivo. New severe clashes with alternating success flared up between the Croatian units which had been charged with security measures, and the bands, with the bands mostly gaining the upper hand. The Croats were thrust back into a defensive operation, with heavy casualties. Nevertheless, they were able to retake Rogatica from the insurgents on February 17.

The insurgents were once more active around Banja Luka and in the area between Bos. Brod and Prijedor. Croatian counter-measures remained ineffective. Hardly back in their garrison the troops of the 718th Infantry Division had to come once more to the aid of the Croats, while the three regional defense battalions which had remained in Croatia were tied by their security tasks to the vital Zagreb-Belgrade railroad, and in the industrial districts.

The situation around Prijedor became especially serious as the Croatian garrison there did not appear quite dependable. Elements of the 923rd Regional Defense Battalion which had been employed for the protection of the ore production were attacked by the insurgents around the middle of February near Prijedor and cut off. Their provisioning was only possible by Croatian aircraft.

The Commander in Serbia, General of Artillery Bader, immediately ordered units of the 718th and 704th Infantry Divisions to move out of East Bosnia to Prijedor. The intervention of these German reinforcements could not be immediately carried out since the transportation of our troops was only possible on a few efficient railroads, via Srm. Mitrovica-Bos. Brod as far as Dubica, and in addition was delayed by heavy snowfall. In such a situation the Wehrmacht Commander Southeast urged the Croatian army command to order out all Croatian troops available in the area of Prijedor for the relief of the encircled German garrison. The Italian Second Army also offered the support of the Italian battalion stationed in Sanski Most.

On February 18 the German reinforcements which had arrived first in Bos. Dubica were committed jointly with about eight Croatian companies against Prijedor. They advanced over heights deep in snow south of Bos. Dubica, but were only able to gain ground slowly against the enemy which fought stubbornly in delaying actions. Further German reinforcements arrived. On the 23rd after continued weak resistance the volunteer corps retreated from the high terrain on both sides of the advance road. On the following day our troops met renewed resistance on the western edge of the Kozara Mountains. On February 27 they finally reached Prijedor which was harassed by the bandits, and extricated the encircled regional defense battalions.

The destructive guerrilla war continued near Prijedor in the mountain country east of Sarajevo, near Rogatica, Braca and Sokolac, between Bosna and Spreca near Doboj and Zvornik on the Drina. By March there was still no peace. On March 10 the rebels attacked a German truck convoy from Mostar near Stolac in the Italian zone of occupation killing 29 German soldiers, wounding 12 and capturing 45. Two Italian companies from Stolac hurried to the aid of their hard-pressed allies. The rebel volunteer corps—they called themselves "Partisans of the National Liberation"—also achieved success in the month of March in Herzegovina by their surprise attacks on Italian supply convoys and security battalions. Towards the end of March in the area east of Sarajevo between Praza and Rogatica "Proletarian" bands from Montenegro were crowding in and reinforcing the volunteer corps. Reinforcements of rebels from Old Serbia were also confirmed here. The volunteer corps also developed lively activity in the "four countries' corner" of Serbia, Montenegro, Herzegovina and Bosnia near Goražde-Visegrad. In the Ozren Mountains, in the west Bosnian area, from Banja Luka as far as Sisak in the Frušta Gora, the centers of unrest continued to exist. Our troops maintained communication from Bos. Brod to the industrial centers north of Sarajevo directly through the region affected by the revolt. German and Croatian units fought with alternating success against the insurgents.

A change in the aggravated situation was not to be expected before the execution of the large encirclement operation in Bosnia which had been agreed upon by the Wehrmacht Commander Southeast and the Italian Second Army in Sisak after lengthy deliberations.

3. Development of the Situation in Serbia
January to March 1942

When the Bulgars at the beginning of January occupied the Old Serbian territory, Nedić raised objections with the German occupation powers against these imperative measures. A strike seemed imminent on account of the entry of the Bulgarians. On the German side, it was resolved to take energetic measures against this. Consideration was given to the possibility of taking into custody the members of the Serbian provisional government if the occasion arose. The Commander in Serbia believed that the Nedić government must be maintained in spite of the crisis created by the entry of the Bulgars, and this conception also coincided with that of the Wehrmacht Commander Southeast: "Serbia is a conquered land, and the provisional government set up by the German occupation powers has to obey but not abdicate." The change of position of the troops in Serbia necessitated at the beginning of January the transport of three regional defense battalions from Croatia. Regional Defense Battalion 924 was posted to Šabac; at the end of the mopping up operations in East Bosnia, the 447th Regional Defense Battalion went to Belgrade in order to take over the security tasks on the railroad to Misak. The third regional defense battalion which had been asked for Serbia was requested by the German General in Zagreb as garrison for the Croatian capital in view of the German interests which had to be protected there.

After the 342nd Infantry Divison had moved out, all the units of the 704th Infantry Division in north Serbia were occupied by the numerous tasks. The Commander in Serbia intended to use two battalions of the 714th Infantry Division, which were employed for the protection of the Belgrade-Lapova railroad, for the security of the industrial plants in Sr. Mitrovica and Raška. The 741st Infantry Regiment of the 714th Infantry Division which had to take over the zone of occupation in northwest Serbia in place of the 342nd Infantry Division, had to set up garrisons in Valjevo, Lajkovac, Obrenovac and Loznica. The 737th Infantry Regiment of the 717th Infantry Division which, after the departure of the 113th Infantry Division, had secured the eastern Morava area, had to remain in Užice and Požega and were to be attached to the units of the 714th Infantry Division. The 717th Infantry Division, without the 737th Infantry Regiment, the 4th Battalion of the 670th Artillery Regiment, the 717th Engineer Company and elements of the 717th Signals Company was intended as replacements for the 164th Infantry Division which was to be transferred to Crete, from the area of Salonika which was denuded of troops. The majority of the two half divisions of the 15th Wave remaining in Serbia and the 718th Infantry Division in Croatia, had to be employed to secure the industrial area important to the war economy. Whatever troops remained were to be held in readiness as mobile reserve for combatting the insurgents. The OKW declared itself in agreement with the intention of moving the majority of the 717th Infantry Division from south Serbia to Salonika, inasmuch as the maintaining of peace and order seemed assured.

After the last major operations of the 342nd and 113th Infantry Divisions the bands in Old Serbia had withdrawn into inaccessible mountains. In the region south of Valjevo and in the Zlatibor mountain range south of Užice, a rather large insurgent group appeared to have assembled in connection with the growing insurgent movement in Bosnia. Towards the end of the month sabotage acts and surprise attacks increased in Serbia, especially in the Bulgarian zone of occupation, in the area around Niš and near Leskovac and Kuršumlije increasing bandit activity was perceptible. In local operations often lasting days units of the 714th Infantry Division tracked down the insurgents in their hide-outs near Valjevo and inflicted considereable losses.

The Bulgarian occupation troops which had been directed by the Wehrmacht Commander Southeast to take more action, successfully carried out in February the mopping up operations requested by the Wehrmacht Commander Southeast. Bitter struggles flared up between Pečanac units and insurgents near Prokuplje.

The terror bands suffered the following losses:

From September 1 to January 15, 1942, enemy losses were a total of 20,000 dead including those shot as reprisal measures. From December 26, 1941 to January 5th, 1942: 504 dead and 50 prisoners.

From February 16, 1942 to March 20, 1942: killed in battle 1,983, killed in reprisal measures, 1,557 (including Croatia).

From February 16 to March 20 German troop losses in Serbia and Bosnia amounted to 37 fallen in battle, 65 wounded and 45 missing.

In the same period the Croats lost: 75 dead and 305 wounded. The Bulgarians lost 15 dead and 13 wounded and finally the Serbian auxiliary police lost 15 dead and 13 wounded.

The Serbian Auxiliary Gendarmerie and both the Serbian and Russian factory guards had acquitted themselves well in the past month. The Serbian Police was renamed the "Serbian State Guard."

Following the proposal of the Wehrmacht Commander Soitheast the OKW on February 19 decreed the amalgamation of the staffs of the Commander in Serbia and the LXV Corps Command, into one staff of the "Commanding General and Commander in Serbia."

As the Spring approached, the flaring up of new large scale revolts, secretly prepared by agents and with British gold can be reckoned with in the territories of Old Serbia and Croatia occupied by our troops. In view of the imminent decisive battles in the east, there could be no thought of the transfer of German reinforcements. Nevertheless peace and order in the Balkans and the protection of supply lines through this territory to Greece and North Africa must be guaranteed. The new directives for combatting the insurgents decreed by the Wehrmacht Commander Southeast on March 19 decreed that all means were to be used which would lead to success. Every regiment in Serbia had to be allotted a fixed area and a pursuit area. Every action of the insurgents was to be rendered impossible by continued patrols even in quiet areas, by current operations and by sudden actions for the purpose of disarming. Initiative, effective action and the most severe and vigorous measures even against prisoners was demanded of all soldiers. In no case may negotiations be entered into with the enemy.[11]

THE ABBAZIA DISCUSSIONS
AND THE RESULTING JOINT OPERATIONS

The modest support which the Italians had given to the first joint German-Italian-Croatian mopping up operation in Croatia in January 1942 caused the Wehrmacht Commander Southeast to approach the OKW on January 21 with the request for a "corresponding political influence" on the Italian allies and "the appointment of a leader in Croatia who would be made responsible for the maintenance of ordered conditions in Croatia." On January 29 the Wehrmacht Commander Southeast once more proposed to the OKW a unified high command for all German, Italian, and Croatian troops for a new mopping up operation, and in a memorandum of February 5, he again stated the necessity for "creating a unified high command in Croatia for suppressing the unrest there."

Suggestions of the Chief of the OKW for a conference

The numerous urgent reports of the Wehrmacht Commander Southeast and of other military officials, especially the German General in Zagreb, concerning the critical development of conditions in the Southeast, directed the attention of the OKW at the turn of the year, more and more to this important military-political area. On February 4 the Chief of the OKW, Field Marshal Keitel, wrote to the Chief of the General Staff of the Italian Wehrmacht, Generaloberst Cavallero, and noted that from a report of the German military representative in Rome, General von Rintelen, he had gathered that the High Command (Commando Supremo) also regarded the situation in Croatia as unsatisfactory.

He too was of the opinion that unified and energetic measures must be taken in the former Yugoslav territory in order finally to break the backbone of the insurgent movement. Field Marshal Keitel then explained further: "With the present straining of its forces on the East front, Germany can only establish limited fighting forces in the Balkans, and must lay greater value on the fact that peace reigns in the areas important for the war economy and the transport lanes remain secured. This end can only be attained however if an offensive mopping up operation according to unified points of view, is carried out now in the whole of Croatia, since experiences up until now have shown that in view of the expanse and the difficulties of the terrain only unsatisfactory results can be -achieved with independent actions. The military power for the carrying out of such a mopping up operation was available with the concentration of the Italian,

Croatian and German forces and would guarantee certain success if measures were taken militarily and politically according to unified points of view." Field Marshal Keitel proposed that "the Italian, Croatian and German command authorities in question receive instruction to work out by personal discussion a joint basis for their further action."

"The discussions must establish the conditions for the carrying out of a coordinated, major mopping up operation for the purpose of annihilating the insurgents and especially to regulate the details of the measures along the demarcation line in this connection. On the other hand, the political measures connected with the military mopping up operation must be placed on a uniform basis." Field Marshal Keitel laid special emphasis on the unified and strict carrying out of the police action which was to be taken in connection with the military mopping up action, because experience up until now had shown that the insurgents evaded military attack and after a district had been combed by our troops, the revolts flared up again. "In addition to these purely police and military measures, it appears to me that the military-political methods which have been applied until now in Croatia are in need of scrutiny. In my opinion the prerequisites for arriving at an amicable agreement with the insurgents do not exist. The continuation of the present uncertain situation prevents any consolidation of the Croatian state and in the long run must lead to its dissolution.

"Passive endurance of the intrigues of the Panslavs, Četniks, and Communists strengthens these forces in view of the limited powers of the Croatian government and can suddenly become a danger to the whole Balkan situation. Therefore everything must be accomplished both militarily and politically in order to strenghten the Croatian government to support energetically its measures against the insurgents and to help it in the building up of its power."[1]

Estimate of the situation by General Roatta

The new commander of the Italian Second Army, General Roatta had in the meantime expressed his opinion on the ideas of a joint action of the Allies (Axis) against the insurgents. On January 26 he received the leader of the German liaison staff with his army, Colonel Rohrbach for a preliminary discussion and expressed the opinion that a serious situation would arise in the Spring, if elimination of the unrest did not occur before then. Moreover he declared himself for a joint and simultaneous action by the Italians, Germans, Bulgarians, and Croatians, with the object of destroying the centers of revolt by concentrated attacks. Then all secondary centers would automatically disintegrate. Such an action would be the best and the most enduring. Independent actions held out very little promise, since after their conclusion the insurgents came together again sooner or later.

To be sure, General Roatta hinted also at the possibility of withdrawing all Italian units to the Dinarian Alps and the establishing of a few strongly fortified garrisons, somewhat similar to medieval castles. Defense must then be limited to the main highways; all the captured areas would have to be given up. General Roatta stated that this action would not, in fact, lead to a pacification of the country but would only spare the Italian troops heavy losses.

A further possibility would be a compromise with the Serbian population to a larger extent than previously and if necessary at the expense of the Croatian state. To a lesser extent the procedure already directed by our administrative office with the consent of the Army had held good. General Roatta thought that only by this procedure, especially in the southern sector, had it been possible to maintain small exposed Italian garrisons without fighting. From the beginning however this proposal would be frustrated for political reasons by the resistance of the Croatian government. Finally there was still a further possibility, said General Roatta, which was "to hunger between two piles of hay like a donkey, which could not make up its mind from which pile of hay to eat."

The statements of General Roatta were indicative of the Italian tendencies. He thought that it had been a mistake to create Croatia, a state that basically was hostile towards Italy. It would have been better to have regarded the whole of the Balkans as enemy territory for the duration of the war, and to have acted accordingly. Then one would not have needed to act with one's gloves on as one had to now. Each Balkan state would have had greater hopes for the future, according to its correct behavior, of a larger Bulgaria, a restored Yugoslavia, or a larger Croatia or an enlarged Hungary. He himself had no scruples about influencing the nations concerned with generous promises which one did not need to keep later. For example, one could easily have promised Graz and Klagenfurt to Croatia.[2]

To the allusion of Colonel Rohrbach that such behavior would be questionable and would bring great difficulties in its train, General Roatta gave no reply. On the contrary, the Italian General continued: He would never have had any scruples, and would have said so both in writing and orally if for example France had been promised Sicily in order to obtain the right to march through Tunisia. It would have been very easy to have found a reason to change this promise later on. He could even imagine that one might hire a few gangsters for the purpose of making an attempt on the life of an Italian statesman at a given time on French territory. Then a new situation would be created which would give one a free hand once more."

The Wehrmacht Commander could not agree in any way to such conceptions. There was no doubt that the real reason for the negotiations of the Italians with the insurgents was the former's unwillingness to fight;"Such methods," the Wehrmacht Commander Southeast informed the German representative with the Italian Second Army, "must be strictly refused as far as we are concerned. Experience has shown that no results were achieved as far as the insurgents were concerned by demonstrating sympathy and tolerance." The Italian Second Army had to be influenced in this sense, for in the long run the German troops were the mourners who had to correct the sins of others."

How little the passive behavior of the Italians had changed since General Roatta had taken over the Second Army, was reported by the Wehrmacht General on February 10. "The revolt is increasing in the whole army area. Until now the Italians had done practically nothing towards the suppression of the revolt. Through the change in command the planned major operations Foča-Goražda had been delayed. An operation at the end of February in the area northeast of Gospic had been planned as the first action, further actions could scarcely be expected henceforth before the beginning of March. Italian-Croatian relations had suffered no crisis through the change of command. At the moment negotiations were taking place between the leaders of the Serbian insurgents and the Moslems for the pacification of South Bosnia, Herzegovina and Montenegro without fighting. The setting up of negotiations with the insurgents seemed to have been ordered directly by General Roatta. The rebels demanded weapons and the evacuation of Bosnia by German and Croatian troops. Italians were to take over in their place."

At the conclusion of this report Colonel Rohrbach pointed out the large number of English agents and English propaganda in the part of Croatia occupied by the Italians. Colonel General Cavallero declared himself in agreement with the proposal of Field Marshal Keitel for a joint mopping up operation, but he desired an Italian high command. The Chief of the OKW replied in a letter of February 20 to the German General at the Headquarters of the Italian Wehrmacht: "I have no objection to a temporary Italian high command for the suppression of the insurgents in the Serbo-Croatian area, provided that the guarantee exists for an energetic military operation, previously agreed upon in detail.

Colonel General Cavallero requested that the discussions which had been proposed by Field Marshal Keitel concerning the planned joint combatting of the revolt in Croatia, be held in the headquarters of the Italian Second Army in Susak. Field Marshal Keitel commissioned the Wehrmacht Commander Southeast on February 19 to represent the OKW at these negotiations in Susak, the time of which was to be agreed upon between the General Staff of the Italian Wehrmacht and the German General in Rome.

Basis for the discussion

The aim of the OKW set forth on December 15, 1941 was to form the basis for this agreement: "To burn out the insurgent territory through the increased use of troops of the Axis powers in the shortest possible time, since in view of the situation in the East not more than two German security divisions could finally be left in the former Yugoslavia and those mainly for the protection of the installations important for our war economy." On February 23 the Wehrmacht Commander Southeast received the following directives from the OKW: "The discussions were to be limited to the discussion of military measures, political questions were to be avoided, the main imperative was to bring the military directives of the Italian Second Army into agreement with those of the Wehrmacht Commander Southeast. The aim of the discussions must be to secure the coordination of the German-Italian-Bulgarian-Hungarian troops with respect to space and time. On the other hand a subordination of German troops under an Italian high command is not contemplated." A subordination of Croatian troops under Italian command if necessary, was alluded to by the OKW.[3]

To the question posed by the OKW as to whether in the interest of a unified treatment of all questions in the Southeast, the Croats as well as the Bulgarians should be asked to send a representative to these discussions, the Wehrmacht Commander Southeast replied in the negative as far as the Bulgarians were concerned in view of the Italian-Bulgarian differences regarding the border in Albania.[4]

After the Italians had agreed to March 2-3 in Susak as the time for these discussions as proposed by the Wehrmacht Commander Southeast, and the Croats had also declared themselves, agreed to take part in the joint operations, General of Engineers Kuntze, together with the Ia,* General Staff Major Macher, and the Qul,* General Staff Major v. Winning departed on February 29 for Belgrade. On the next day the principles of the agreement to be taken up with the Italians and the Croats were discussed with the Commanding General and Commander in Serbia, General of Artillery Bader.

---

* Ia — German military abbreviation for Chief of Staff.
  Qul — Similarly, Chief of Quartermaster Division.

From the diary of the Wehrmacht Commander Southeast

The plan of these conference principles was worked out during the journey to Belgrade. In this diary the proposals of the Wehrmacht Commander Southeast were based on the following principles:

Serbia: After the destruction last November of the strongest group of forces, until now Colonel Mihailović who had made the western Morava valley the life line of his main insurgent territory, there no longer existed in Serbia today a connected insurgent area. In Croatia two large centers of unrest had existed, where it had not been possible to capture the enemy, namely in East Bosnia in the area behind the Bosna, Sarajevo, Drina and Tuzla."

In the middle of January a joint action of German and Croatian troops was successful in effecting the recapture of the area around Sarajevo. At the moment there were groups of insurgents on the Ozren Mountains and northeast of Sarajevo in the area of the Romanja Mountains. An influx of Montenegrin bands had taken place from the Italian territory via Foča and Višegrad. The second area of unrest in West Bosnia, in the area between Banja Luka-Sava-Kostajnica-Topusk, is at the moment the strongest center of unrest.

In the Italian zone of occupation, the mountains and passes along the German-Italian demarcation line were mainly in the hands of the insurgents, as far as the Wehrmacht Commander Southeast could perceive. Here connected centers of unrest in the areas Dubrovnik-Višegrad-demarcation line-Konjica-Mostar-Bugojne-demarcation line-Vargar Vakuf-Livno, further around Ogmin-Topusk and north of Gospic' were recognizable. The center of unrest in the area of Dubrovnik-Višegrad-demarcation line-Konjica-Mostar is of special significance for the joint conduct of the war, since it separates the Axis powers and thereby gives the insurgents the opportunity of gaining access via the demarcation line to the insurgent groups in East Bosnia and the Zlatibor mountains in Serbia.

Forces available:

    I. German forces:

        In Serbia three security divisions each with two regiments, five regional defense battalions and one police battalion. Operational area: North and northwest Serbia. In Croatia, one security division, two regional defense battalions, all German forces are committed with combat tasks.

    II. Bulgarian forces:

        Three Bulgarian divisions secure the area around Niš. Even with regard to the Albanian question they are not to be considered for cooperation on the German-Italian demarcation line.

III. Croatian forces:

Three corps, six divisions, 16 regiments. Since the army is only now being built up, its fighting value is limited. Figures regarding auxiliary forces, police and Ustasha are lacking.

IV. Italian forces:

Second Army: 4 corps with 12 divisions
Ninth Army: 2 corps with 5 divisions, among which are one mountain and one medium mountain division (Mittelgebirgsdiv.)

Focal point of the Italian Second Army in the second sector of the Italian zone of occupation. Another six divisions predominately committed for the protection of the coastal communications in the vicinity of the coast. Along the demarcation line security only in the form of guards.

The Ninth Army had transferred the 5th Mountain Division into the area around Plevlje, two divisions lay in the vicinity of the coast, one division in the Albanian border region.

Conduct of the war:

The prerequisite for the conquering of the country is the destruction of the large centers of unrest, in which the enemy had been able to hold his ground until now by planned strikes. The most dangerous centers of unrest are: East Bosnia and the adjoining insurgent area to the south, north of Dubrovnik, West Bosnia, both sides of the demarcation line.

The suppression of the unrest in both these areas is likewise a prerequisite for the solution of the further tasks of the German, Italian, and Croatian Wehrmacht. It is therefore to be unified in a joint action. The German, as well as the Italian and Croatian command can only free limited forces for a joint attack. Therefore it was a question of concentrating at the same time the available forces of the three armies and of guaranteeing their unified command.

To attain this the Wehrmacht Commander Southeast proposed the following:

1) The situation in East Bosnia and in the adjoining insurgent territory north of Dubrovnik would be cleared up by the concentration of German, Italian and Croatian troops.

Task of the German High Command: Gaining control and mopping up the area south of Sarajevo, especially the mountain passes near Višegrad and Paraćin. Following in a mopping up according to plan with the aim of gaining complete freedom of movement for the Italian troops in the area northwest of Plevlje and northeast of Mostar. Accordingly, liaison with the German combat unit Sarajevo is to be secured constantly.

2) The situation in West Bosnia will be cleared up by the concentration of Italian and Croatian forces.

Tasks of Italian High Command: Reopening of the most important traffic lanes and the passes across the demarcation line Bogojno, south of Jajce, east of Klin, north of Sanski Most and near Otoce. Thereafter mopping up both sides of the demarcation line, with the aim of keeping open the passes named and thereby securing the possibility of continued operation.

3) The clearing up of the situation north of Gospic is a task for the Italians, just as the maintaining of peace and order in Serbia is one for the Germans.

Preliminary discussions in Zagreb

After the Wehrmacht Commander Southeast had discussed these principles in Belgrade, he left on the evening of February 20, with his staff and with the Commanding General and Commander in Serbia, for Zagreb, in order to continue there the preliminary discussions with the Croats. Ambassador Benzler accompanied the German military leaders on this journey. In Zagreb the first discussions took place on the 27th with the German General in Zagreb (General von Glaise Horstenau), German Ambassador Kasche and with Dr. Veesenmayer who had been called in to the discussions at the request of the Foreign Office in Berlin to act as political adviser.

Ambassador Kasche telegraphed the Foreign Office in Berlin on February 28 regarding the results of this preliminary discussion:

"Discussions took place yesterday evening. Unanimity resulted. The contemplated military discussions with the Italians and the Croats were regarded as useful by all concerned. It was agreed that all political possibilities should be exploited in order to relieve the operation of all military forces. This would be especially possible with regard to the relations between Serbia and Croatia."

Ambassador Benzler stressed: "The planned military operation in Croatia must take into account that no new political difficulties arise for the Nedic' government." It was acknowledged that the frontier between Croatia and Serbia could not be discussed.

My viewpoint was: With regard to the cooperation of the Italians no tasks or demands may be given to the Italians for the occupation of any (Croatian) areas. The area around Prijedor-Banja Luka is important for us as regards the war economy and also racially and politically. The suppression of the insurgents here is urgent. Even the cooperation of weaker German units is desired. No objections will be raised against Italian command in other operations if the Croats are agreed.

On February 28 the preliminary talks between the Wehrmacht Commander Southeast, the Commanding General and Commander in Serbia and the German General in Zagreb, on the one hand, and of the General Staff of the Croatian army (Major General Laxa) on the other were continued. At the discussion with the Chief of the General Staff of the Croatian army, on the morning of the 28th, the Wehrmacht Commander Southeast made known the order which had been given to him by the OKW to combat the revolt in Croatia, as well as his own operational plan. He described the German conception of the situation in Croatia and Serbia, and then discussed his intentions:

1) German forces around Sarajevo had to occupy the mountain passes around Sarajevo and Tarčin and at the same time to safeguard the industrial plants. The Italians were to be asked to reach these mountain passes simultaneously from their zone, and in such a manner that they advance with strong forces along the existing roads in order to mop up from north to south, the region through which they had advanced. For this operation the support of 10 to 12 Croatian battalions was considered necessary.

2) Operation Banja Luka.
In addition to the Sarajevo operation, the insurgent area in the region of Banja Luka was to be mopped up of insurgents at the same time. For this purpose only the regional defense battalion in Prijedor was available for German forces. The support of this operation by 10 to 12 Croatian battalions was also deemed necessary. The Italians were to be asked for support in the same manner as in the Sarajevo operation.

Concerning the result of the discussion with the Croats, the Wehrmacht Commander reported further to the OKW:

The representation of the Croatian Wehrmacht up until now was confirmed. Unconditional cooperation of the German-Croatian command and troops was secured. Croatian command prepared, in a few insurgent areas, to subordinate itself also to the Italian high command. The Croats also recognized the importance of police actions which had to follow up immediately the regaining of insurgent territory. Mutual experiences have confirmed that to regain the main insurgent territories a period of at least 4-6 weeks would be necessary.[5]

Deliberations at Abbazia

On March 1 the Wehrmacht Commander Southeast, with his staff officers departed from Zagreb for Fiume (Rijeka), for the joint discussions with the Italians. Marshal Kvaternik was represented on this occasion by his Chief of General Staff, Major General Laxa. At the request of the Italians, at first only discussions between the German and Italian representatives took place in the headquarters of the Italian Second Army at Abbazia (Opatija) near Fiume. Those present were:

> General Ambrosio (Chief of the General Staff of the Italian Army),
> General of Engineers Kuntze (Wehrmacht Commander Southeast),
> General von Glaise Horstenau (German General in Zagreb)
> General Roatta (Commander in Chief, Italian Second Army),
> General of Artillery Bader (Plenipotentiary Commanding General in Serbia),
> General Gandini (Italian High Command),
> Major General Rintelen (German General at the Headquarters of the Italian Wehrmacht), and the accompanying staff officers.

Operational suggestions of the Wehrmacht Commander Southeast

General Ambrosio greeted the participators at the conference and declared the aim of the meeting was to arrive at an understanding for a joint operation to suppress the insurgents in Croatia.

The Wehrmacht Commander Southeast spoke first about the overall situation. In Serbia there were no longer any large insurgent areas, whereas in Croatia two rather large centers of revolt existed. One was between the Bosna and Drina rivers, and the other near Banja Luka, around Kožara (Kozara), on the Priseka heights (Samarica), as far as Petrova Gora (in the Italian zone southwest of Vojnić-Topusk). At the present time this insurgent territory was being penetrated by five German battalions attempting to reach Prijedor and take the Bos. Novi-Kostajnica railroad. Afterwards these German forces would be transferred to East Bosnia, leaving one regional defense battalion for the protection of the mines at Prijedor. Then it was intended to mop up the area south and southeast of Sarajevo with the 718th Infantry Division and about eight Croatian battalions at the same time holding the Praca line, south of Zvornik. The Tarčin, Trnovo and Rogatica passes on the demarcation line were to be taken in order to set up liaison with the Italians there and thus cut off the insurgents in the Italian occupation zone from the Italians in East Bosnia. For this purpose the German and Croatian forces on hand would suffice, and could at the same time safeguard the industrial area and the railroads in East Bosnia. If liaison with the Italian troops situated south of the demarcation line is secured, then it is planned to mop up the Drina bend near Rogatica.

In the area of Banja Luka, the Wehrmacht Commander Southeast continued, there were at the moment about 10 Croatian battalions holding the lines of communication, but not the Prijeder-Bos. Novi railroad. The main insurgent territory lay in the Kožara and Priseka (Samarica). The Croatian forces did not suffice for the mopping up of the insurgent territory in West Bosnia, especially with their weak fighting qualities. For this reason he had suggested to the Croatian army command in Zagreb that the mopping up of this area be handed over to the Italian Second Army. He suggested the following operations to the Italian Second Army:

1) Putting down of the revolt in the Petrova Gora (Italian occupation zone)
2) Putting down of the revolt in the Priseka (Samarica) and Kozara (German occupation zone)

Counter suggestions of General Ambrosio

General Ambrosio had other plans. He proceeded from the viewpoint that "only Croatia will be considered" (therefore not the revolt situation in the Italian zone of occupation). To the great surprise of the Wehrmacht Commander Southeast he stated that "according to an agreement between Field Marshal Keitel and the Italian High Command, the Italian Second Army will have command of the joint operation.*

General Ambrosio stressed: "The main question is that the whole operation will be unified, and that our own forces will not be split. The center of the insurgent area lies around Sarajevo, therefore we must begin in East Bosnia. As far as possible one can combat other points of the revolt at the same time, but only in a subsidiary manner."

After these opening remarks of General Ambrosio, the Wehrmacht Commander Southeast amplified: If two Italian divisions advanced from the south (towards the mountain passes Tarcin-Trnovo and Praca) and then came through from north to south (the Italian zone

---

* In the directives of the OKW for the discussions with the Italians, published on February 23, the Wehrmacht Commander Southeast was informed: "A subordination of German troops under Italian command is not contemplated." However, in order to meet the wishes of the Italians, the Chief of the OKW had promised the Italian High Command a transient limited subordination of German units under the Italian Second Army. After discussion with the Fuehrer the German General with the Headquarters of the Italian Wehrmacht was directed to explain to Colonel General Cavallero a change in the Feburary 27 agreement: "The right of disposition over German units in Serbia and Croatia, the designation of the time and extent of their commitment, in addition the consent to a joint action against the insurgents is incumbent only on the Wehrmact Commander Southeast. During the execution of such a jointly fixed action there is no objection against a subordination, limited in time, of the committed units under the Italian Second Army."[6]

of occupation south of Sarajevo) the Germans would be able to exe-
cute the operation with one German division and the Croatian battalions. A further German division could be brought up from the east
to block off [on the Drina]. The Wehrmacht Commander Southeast
made the proposal to transfer the carrying out of this operation to
General of the Artillery Bader, who knew the conditions there so
well and who had to conform as far as possible to the directives of
the Italian Second Army.

General Ambrosio declared himself in agreement with this and
stressed once more the necessity of a unified high command over the
whole operation by the Italian Second Army. "After the operation it
will be necessary to leave rather large and also smaller Italian garrisons as police in the insurgent territory until Croatia can provide sufficient police forces. Because of this the demarcation line will be dis-
continued. An eventual shifting of the demarcation line must, if the
occasion arises, remain reserved for a later ruling. According to a letter of Field Marshal Keitel parallel directives for police and political
questions are to be assumed. General Ambrosio declared that no
connections existed on the part of the Italians with the insurgents.

The Wehrmacht Commander Southeast indicated that the operation around Banja Luka must also start as soon as possible. General
Ambrosio replied that with the few available troops it was not possible to carry out both operations (in east Bosnia and in west Bosnia)
thoroughly at the same time, and therefore it was to be arranged
that the second operation (west Bosnia) should directly follow the
first (east Bosnia). The Wehrmacht Commander Southeast thought
that the conclusion of the first operation could not be expected before May. If however the Italians could release 3 or 4 divisions both
operations would be possible at the same time and both main insurgent centers could be eliminated simultaneously.*

Results of the discussions

On the morning of March 3, the Croatian representative, General
Laxa also took part in the discussions conducted by General Ambrosio.
It was agreed that an operational group, consisting of one German
division (718th Infantry Division), three Italian divisions, and all avail-
able Croatian units (8-10 battalions), commanded by General of
Artillery Bader under the high command of the Italian Second Army,
General Roatta, should at first destroy the rebels in east Bosnia.

---

* From the notes of the Wehrmacht Commander Southeast Ia on the discussions in Abbazia.

The Italians declared that sufficient forces were not available for the simultaneous joint suppression of the insurgents in west Bosnia too. As General Ambrosio reported, the Italian Second Army could only release these three divisions for the joint operation, in view of the revolt in the Italian zone of occupation.* Therefore the two operations in east Bosnia (at the "four countries corner"—Bosnia, Herzegovina, Montenegro, Serbia) and in west Bosnia: Banja Luka, Sava, Topusk, Ogulin, Enij, Ljig, Vranić should take place after each other and not simultaneously as the Wehrmacht Commander had stated. The Wehrmacht Commander must of necessity agree to this because of the importance of east Bosnia to the Serbian area. In this manner the total time needed was to be doubled—the reinforcement of the insurgents in west Bosnia was also probable until it could be entered at the conclusion of the operation in east Bosnia.

The following starting points were contemplated for the joint operation in east Bosnia: For the German and Croatian troops the line south of Tarcin, Trnova pass, Praća, Rogatica, Sokolac, Han Pijesak, Vlasenica, Drina (south of Zvornik). For the Italian troops on the south front the line Kalinovik, Hoban on the east bank of the Drina-Višegrad and on the southwest front of the demarcation line.

Although the Germans and the Croatians demanded that the operation begin as soon as possible, the Italians declared that they would not be in a position before the middle of April to fall in from the starting point for the joint operation against east Bosnia. They needed this time to reinforce the units which were intended for the operations, to carry out the necessary deployment movements and to destroy the enemy forces which were on the approach roads. This was not possible before the middle of April. Based upon previous experience, they also considered the arrival of milder weather and the thaw as an absolute prerequisite for the successful execution of the operation.

---

* On February 24 the Leader of the German Liaison Staff with the Italian Second Army, Colonel Rohrbach informed the Wehrmacht Commander Southeast by radio: "Ex officio talks with General Roatta in the evening of 2/23 show that the Italian Second Army had reckoned with reinforcements from German troops for a major operation. The supply situation of the Italians was already difficult, therefore the transfer of further Italian troops to Croatia would apparently not be considered. Liaison Staff with the Italian Second Army Ia No. 107/42 top secret of 2.24.42 and Wehrmacht Commander Southeast Ia No. 577/42 top secret of 2.25.42.

The operation in west Bosnia was to be started immediately following the mopping up in East Bosnia. At the conclusion of the whole operation, police actions (mopping up actions) were to be carried out by all units. With the continued pacification of East Bosnia, the Croatian administration was set up once more.

When at this point the question of the demarcation line after the end of the operation was brought up by the Italians, the German General in Rome, General von Rintelen, pointed out that according to the agreement between the OKW and the Commando Supremo, this disputed matter was to be left to a later ruling, if this should be necessary. No further discussions took place.

On March 3 the agreements reached were taken down in the minutes. Essentially the 12 points of the protocol attested:

1) Purpose of the operation: "Final mopping up of the insurgents in Croatia."

2) Enemy situation:

   a) In Serbia there are no strong enemy groups.

   b) In Croatia northeast of the demarcation line, in addition to smaller enemy groups, there are two strong centers of unrest between the Bosna and Drina rivers and in the area Banja Luka and Petrova Gora.

   c) In addition there are the groups of insurgents southwest of the demarcation line.

3) Forces available for the operations:

   a) Italian forces: Three divisions as well as strong aerial forces.

   b) German forces: One division.

   c) Croatian forces: 8-10 battalions.

4) Command: "The Commander in Chief of the Italian Second Army, General Roatta was intended for the unified command of the operations. He will take over the command of the operation, when the units reach the starting off points."

5) General operational plan: "The available troops will be committed first in East Bosnia. Later the operation will extend in a northwesterly direction. The operational plan will be agreed upon by the Commander in Chief of the Italian Second Army and with General Bader. General Bader will be subordinated to the high command of the Italian Second Army and lead the operation himself. For this purpose the German-Italian-Croatian army units intended for the operation are subordinate to him.

6) The operation must be carried out as speedily as possible.

7) April 15 is fixed for the commencement of the operation.

8) The administration (civilian power) in the occupied territories. After the pacification of the individual zones the Croatian civilian authorities will be appointed for administration according to the decision of the Commander in Chief of the Italian Army.

9) During the operation and the following pacification the demarcation line cannot be regarded as such.

10) The signatories of the treaty pledge themselves not to negotiate either with the Četniks or with the Communists.

11) This point regulates the equal treatment of the rebels and the population.

12) The signatories of the pact pledge themselves to exchange their information on the enemy.

Objections of the Croatians to the Sušak Protocol

On March 4 the Wehrmacht Commander Southeast left Fiume. General von Rintelen who had taken part in the deliberations in Abbazia by order of the Chief of the OKW, returned to Rome in order to request via the Commando Supremo the consent of the Duce to the agreement which had been reached. General von Rintelen reported to the OKW that he had gained the impression that the result of the discussions had pleased all participants on the essential points.

The Croats, however, were not satisfied. In particular Point B of the Abbazia protocol had awakened their fears that once the Italians had marched into East Bosnia they would never leave the land, especially Sarajevo. On his return journey from Fiume, the Wehrmacht Commander Southeast visited Marshal Kvaternik in Zabreb. The Croatian Marshal said at that time that as Croatian Wehrmacht Commander in Chief he considered any sojourn of Italian troops in Sarajevo and the industrial area of Tuzla-Zenica as untenable, likewise the carrying out of the operation without any influence of the Croatian government.

Marshal Kvaternik approached Field Marshal Keitel with a request to bring the following to the notice of the Fuehrer: "The Protocol of the discussions which took place on March 3 in Abbazia, concerning the cooperation between the Italian, German and Croatian forces for the final mopping up of the rebels in Croatia, and for the pacification of the insurgent territories in Croatia cannot be accepted for important political, economic and military reasons."

"The above assertion is based on the terrible experience which we had in the II Zone,* in which nine Italian divisions not only could

---

* In this zone—the region of the Dinaric Alps, the so-called "demilitarized zone" the Croats may maintain garrisons but no fortifications or defense installations. The Italians had taken over the military and civilian power as a matter of form.

not carry out the pacification, but the condition there became 100 per cent worse and almost brought about the ruin of our administration and our economy.

"If one wants to help the Croats, then one cannot dictate to us but must ask us where the shoe pinches, and what help we need and where.

"Where and when operations are to be carried out cannot be decided in advance en bloc but only in agreement with the Croatian government.

"At first we propose the thorough mopping up of the territory on the Drina, between Zvornik, Goražde and Foča and further via Kalinovik, Praca, Sokolac and Vlasenica, but under the condition that the whole police and administrative power remains in the hands of the Croats. If military administrative authorities are preferred, then we will militarize the civilian authorities and place them under the command of experienced Croatian officers.

"We reserve for ourselves the right to carry out independent operations in other parts of Croatia, for example in the Kozara Mountains, Majevica Mountains, and Petrova Gora, without having come to any agreement previously with our allies.

"We are completely agreed that during joint actions General of the Artillery Bader, Commanding General and Commander in Serbia, is the Commander of all troops.

"The operational troops of our allies who are committed outside of their demarcation line during the operations, remain in those areas only as long as the Croats wish and no longer.

"The maintaining of the demarcation line is a question of life and death for the Croatian government.

"We are agreed that in the operational zone all Ustasha formations shall be subordinated to the command of General of Artillery Bader.

"The center of unrest in zone II—especially in Herzegovina where the Četniks were masters, is more dangerous and larger than in the rest of Croatia, therefore pacification and destruction in zone II must be a prerequisite for further operations.

"The advance of the Italians on the Sava would even lead to serious unrest in the region north of the Sava, and thereby threaten the whole economy.

"My opinion was, is and remains that the occupation of zone II has not served the joint aims of the Axis and that a further occupation by Italian troops, as well as the taking over of the police and the exclusion of our administrative power, would without doubt result in revolt in Serbia and a loss of prestige for Germany and threaten the Croatian State which must be prevented at all costs.

"Sarajevo and the Croatian 'Ruhr' area which is bounded on the west by the Bosna, on the north by the Sava, on the east by the Zvornik-Vlasenica-Han Pijesak-Romanja Mountains line may not be entered by anyone except the German and Croatian Wehrmacht. This is a political-economic ruling."

This letter, which was handed to the Wehrmacht Commander Southeast during his departure from Zagreb on March 4 *was not allowed to be presented to the Chief of the OKW in a later request of Field Marshal Kvaternik.*

On March 4 in his report on the results of the discussions in Abbazia, the Wehrmacht Commander Southeast requested that at the confirmation of the agreement an effort should be made to limit the presence of Italian troops in the area freed of insurgents around Sarajevo and in the Sarajevo-Tuzla area, so important to the German war economy, to the shortest possible period.[7]

Even the German political representatives in Zagreb expressed their hesitation with regard to a lasting occupation of the remainder of Croatia by the Italians.

Dr. Veesenmayer, who had been sent to Zagreb as adviser in political questions by the Foreign Office in Berlin, believed that owing to the weak offensive power of the Italians, their operation will extend a long way beyond the demarcation line, and this territory will actually come under Italian administration. The danger exists that this may then become a permanent condition and the insurgent movement in Croatia may take on a Panslav character, which would call in question Croatia's existence, and which could only then be maintained by strong military means. With the tense situation that existed between the Croats and the Italians, the Croats looked with sorrow upon the military authority of the Italians over the Croatians. If Sarajevo were under Italian administration for any length of time, the Croats would be especially touchy.

In order to dispel the fear of the Croatian government, that the Italians, once they had marched into Sarajevo would never leave this city, the German Ambassador in Zagreb, Kasche, offered the following supplement to the Abbazia protocol: "The sovereignty of Croatia remains unaffected, the frontiers and the demarcation line remain unchanged. In the pacified territories the internal administration will be taken over as soon as possible by the Croatian authorities. Until that time the employment of Croatian administrative headquarters under the command of the military Commander in Chief is contemplated. Military preparations will not be affected by the necessary political rulings, they will continue."

The German General in Zagreb too tried to find a way out of these inconsistencies and strongly recommended compliance with the wishes of the Croats regarding Sarajevo. In order to dispel the concerns of the Croats, since the Italians could settle down for a long time in the area of Sarajevo and in the industrial area of Tuzla-Vares-Zenica, the German General in Zagreb was commissioned by the OKW on March 6 to suggest to the Croatian government that it place a proposal before the German and Italian high commands. The proposal would be supported by the Germans and handled jointly with the Italians.[8]

In the meantime news of an Italian entry had already leaked out in Sarajevo. These rumors had occasioned a very marked revolt in Sarajevo, the palladium of the whole Moslem world in Bosnia.

On March 14 the Croatian government directed a memorandum concerning the mopping up action in Croatia to the Foreign Office in Berlin, in which it stated:

"The Foreign Ministry of the Independent State of Croatia takes the liberty of making known the Croatian point of view in connection with the discussions which took place in Sušak (Abbazia) on the 3rd of March of this year.

1) The Croatian government receives with pleasure the fundamental thought according to which Italian and German forces are to undertake in cooperation with Croatian forces a radical mopping up of certain regions in Croatia of the Communist and Četnik bands.

2) The sovereignty of the Independent State of Croatia and the exercise of sovereign rights by the Croatian State apparatus however remain completely unlimited by these military actions.

3) The exercise of administration by the Croatian State apparatus cannot be prejudiced by the military actions for the combatting of disturbances.

4) In the areas of unrest, where the internal administration has to be built up again this building will be effected by Croatian administrative headquarters, which will be relieved as soon as possible by regular Croatian civilian administration.

5) The combatting and cutting off of the centers of unrest outside of Croatia, especially in Serbia, Novi Pazar and Montenegro is an essential prerequisite for the success of the operation in Serbia. The Croatian government is of the opinion that the point of view set forth above is appropriate for expediting to a high degree the preparations for the military mopping up action as well as the mopping up actions themselves, especially with regard to the knowledge of the local conditions which had been considered by both the German and Italian forces within the areas fixed by the demarcation line.[9]

To an enquiry of the Wehrmacht Commander Southeast the German General in Zagreb reported:

"In this memorandum it is a question, as far as the Croats are concerned, with regard to a lasting occupation by allied troops, of maintaining the status quo while retaining their own sovereignty. This also concerns especially the continuation of the so-called demarcation line and its present state and thereby also the wish of the Croats that Sarajevo shall be neither attached to the Italian occupation zone nor be maintained continually as an Italian garrison."

Then the German General in Zagreb described the excitement which the rumors of the impending entry of the Italians into Sarajevo had occasioned. He was of the opinion that if there was no thought of withdrawing the German troops out of Croatia, then one should at least comply with the Croatian wishes concerning Sarajevo. As yet there had been no discussion on the conditions after the conclusion of the planned operation. Since one could not do away with the whole male population of the insurgent territory, nor evacuate it, the problem of sufficient supervision of the mopped up areas by troops, gendarmerie and police still remained. With the nine battalions at the moment in the German occupation zone (Croatia), the German Wehrmacht can in no way fulfill this task. It is questionable whether the Croatian army can attain the necessary strength and organization in the course of the summer. No unsettling experiences had occurred until now with the occupation by Italian troops south of the present demarcation line. In view of the strong aversion of all Croats toward the Italians an extension of the Italian zone of occupation would scarcely facilitate a considerable pacification of the situation in this area. Therefore one would also have to reckon with the continuation of the insurgent movement, flaring up sporadically in varying strength at the conclusion of the planned action. It is indeed to be hoped that our German troops will at least hold down to a certain extent the insurgent movement in East Bosnia.[10]

The Joint German-Italian-Croatian Operation in East Bosnia
Preparations for the Joint Operation

At the conclusion of the deliberations in Abbazia, the joint operation was again discussed on March 5 in Belgrade between the Wehrmacht Commander Southeast, the Commanding General and Commander in Serbia and the German General in Zagreb. The Wehrmacht Commander Southeast then went to the Fuehrer Headquarters in order to report to the Chief of the OKW on March 7, the result of the agreement of Abbazia and to request permission for these arrangements. The Fuehrer and also the Duce declared themselves in agreement with the arrangements taken by the Italian Second Army.

On March 16th, two days after the return of the Wehrmacht Commander Southeast to his headquarters at Arsakly near Saloniki, the order arrived from the OKH for the setting up of an operational staff for the Combat Group of General of Artillery Bader. Hereupon the Wehrmacht Commander Southeast commissioned the Commanding General and Commander Serbia with the "preparation and execution of measures which were to be taken by the Germans." Preparations for the new task were to be commenced immediately.

On March 18 Lt. Colonel Pfaffenrott of the General Staff, who was intended for the Chief of the General Staff of the Bader Combat Group arrived in Belgrade and brought the Commanding General and Commander in Serbia[11] the combat directives of the Wehrmacht Commander Southeast for the operation in East Bosnia.

Combat directives of the Wehrmacht Commander Southeast

"Until 4.15, that is until the beginning of the joint German-Italian operation according to Paragraph 7 of the Protocol of Abbazia, continuation of the mopping up in the area north and west of the agreed jump-off position will take place.

"After April 15 occupation, mopping up and pacification of the main insurgent territory Rogatica-south of Zvornik-Vlasenica-Sokolac-Rogatica-Prača-Kalinovik-Plevlje-Višegrad according to the commands of the Italian Second Army.

"As far as the Germans are concerned the prompt sealing off of the Serbian-Croatian border is of especial importance in order to prevent the escape of the insurgents in the Serbian area.

"Guaranteeing of the protection of the installations, stocks and communications important for the German war industry, in the main by Croatian troops.

"Support of the setting up of the Croatian administration according to the definitions of the protocol.

"General of Artillery Bader is subordinate to the Wehrmacht Commander Southeast, and, with the taking over of command according to Paragraph 4, tactically to the Italian Second Army.

"For tasks according to Paragraph 3 the following are subordinated to General of Artillery Bader: the German 718th Infantry Division, elements of the German units committed in Serbia at the proposal of General of Artillery Bader, Croatian units and units according to the previous agreement with the Croatian Wehrmacht command: from

April 15 approximately three Italian divisions according to the command of the Italian Second Army. All these forces would be concentrated under the designation "Combat Group General Bader."[12]

Proposed for the operation of Combat Group General Bader

On March 19 the Commander in Chief of the Italian Second
Army General Roatta, requested the Combat Group Bader, with
reference to the "time already passed" for a "speedy proposal for an
operation" so that the operation could commence on April 15.[13]
Thereupon General of Artillery Bader transmitted by radio on the
same day via the German liaison officer with the Italian Second
Army the following proposal for an operation:

Intention: Destruction of the insurgents in the area Goražde-
Višegrad-Han Pijesak-Sokolac-Praca.

Preparation: one Italian mountain division in and south of the
line Visegrad-Mofjedja, one Italian division in the line Usti-Prača-
Goražde and south of it, one Italian mountain division both sides of
Kalinovik and south of it, a German-Croatian group Trnove, a German regimental group in the line Prača-Sokolac, a German regimental
group Sokolac-Han Pijesak.

Execution: Target of all offensive columns—Rogatica. Italian division on the left flank falls in on 4.15, with its right flank on the road
Kalinovik-Goražde, with a strong right flank via Dobro Polje through
the Drina Valley to the German left flank near Han Pijesak. Time required for the march of the flanks: 3 days.

The discussions at Laibach

Before the operational staff of the Combat Group Bader moved
its headquarters from Belgrade to Sarajevo, General of Artillery Bader
and his Chief of Staff went to Laibach, where the Liaison Officer
with the Italian Second Army, Colonel Rohrbach had suggested a
new discussion with General Roatta. When the allies met there on
March 28 for their deliberations, affairs seemed to have taken a surprising turn.[14] The Italians once more brought up the moot questions of Sarajevo, Croatian administration of the occupied zone, and
also the disturbing question of negotiations with the insurgents. At
the very beginning of the conference, General Roatta caused surprise by the remark that the Croatian State Secretary Vrančić had
informed him that the Croatian government intended to provide the
Četniks in Herzegovina with weapons, if in exchange for them they
would fight against Communists and defend the Croatian border
against Montenegro. After Major General Laxa had admitted that the
Croatian government was still negotiating with the insurgents in

in Herzegovina, General Roatta declared that he considered the German and Italian authorities also authorized to negotiate with the insurgents. Further he confirmed that Article No. 10 of the Protocol of Abbazia, the prohibition of negotiations with the insurgents, had become invalid.[15]

If General Roatta now in a surprising manner announced the intention of negotiating with the insurgents, contrary to the agreement of Abbazia, he was obviously thinking of the Četniks who were hostile to the Croats. To be sure, he wanted to fight the Partisan-Communists unconditionally, but to negotiate with the national Serbian bands for tactical reasons, in order to exclude these for the time being from the fight. He did not recognize any difference between the Četniks in Herzegovina and those in Bosnia, such as was made by the Croats.

After the writing down of the points of discussion, General Roatta said literally: "We are agreed that the Četniks fight against the Communists, and we too will above all fight the Communists. Is it then advisable that instead of exploiting this situation, we advance against both Četniks and Communists at the same time? Thereby we force both parties into the same camp. To me it would appear wiser to do away first with the Communist danger, then once this danger is removed the question of the Četniks can be considered in the second phase. It is obvious that later these [Četniks] must also be removed. It would however be unwise, to create an enemy 10,000, maybe 20,000 strong, at first. In the first phase, "Combatting of Communists," one could reckon on the support of the Četniks, or at least one could keep them out of the struggle."[16]

During the continuation of the discussions on March 29 General Roatta once more brought up the question of negotiating with the insurgents. He was of the opinion that the Communists were hostile to everybody, and under no circumstances was there any question of negotiating with them. The Četniks were indeed hostile to Croatia, but were not enemies of the Axis. Once more the Italian General stressed the usefulness of first negotiating with the Četniks, naturally with the consent of the Croatian government. To a certain extent it was only a question of an armistice. The fight against the Četniks would later be carried out jointly if necessary. Finally Major General Laxa declared himself ready to obtain the consent of the Croatian government to the intended negotiations with the Četniks, and the Commander of the Combat Group Bader had no other alternative but to consent to those intentions, as otherwise no unified command of the Combat Group Bader would have been possible.[17]

General Roatta also opposed the conception of the Croatian government that the taking over of the actual authority in the occupation zones by military offices, would indicate an encroachment on the sovereignty of the Croatian State. He was of the opinion that not only according to German and Italian, but also international custom, the commander of a unit exercised executive power during an operation, at least as far as the operation demanded. The German representative agreed to this conception.

On March 29 Combat Group Bader reported to the Wehrmacht Commander Southeast on the results of the discussions in Laibach:

1) General Roatta had confirmed that the article of the protocol, "Prohibition of negotiations with the insurgents," was no longer valid, after General Laxa had admitted that at the moment the Croatian government was negotiating with the insurgents in Herzegovina.

2) General Roatta amends the operational plan, since it is impossible to provision two divisions on the Foča-Goražde highway. Order for one Italian division via Višegrad, one Italian division via Sarajevo (rail transport), from there to Dobro Polje then as before. German forces approximately as before.

3) Sarajevo to be Italian supply base and air supporting point.[18]

Prohibition against negotiation with insurgents upheld

The Wehrmacht Commander Southeast declared himself in agreement with the result of the discussions in Laibach with regard to the command of the operation.   In no case however could the Wehrmacht Commander Southeast consent to the intention to negotiate with the insurgents, since the execution of the whole operation would be called in question thereby. Moreover this question must be withheld for the decision of the OKW.[19]

On March 30 the Wehrmacht Commander Southeast telegraphed to the German General at the Headquarters of the Italian Wehrmacht in Rome to try to prevent the intentions of General Roatta to negotiate with the rebels to avoid endangering the success of the joint operation.[20] At the same time the Wehrmacht Commander Southeast forced a decision of the OKW when he reported to the latter on April 2 that the agreement had been reached with regard to the carrying out of the operation, but that General Roatta had expressed the firm intention of taking up unconditional combat only against the Partisans (Communists) according to the agreements at Sušak, and of negotiating with the national Serbian bands in order to temporarily keep them out of the struggle. Combatting of national Serbian bands would follow later. The Wehrmacht Commander Southeast considered the intention of General Roatta wrong, and requested that the Commando Supremo take steps to prevent the negotiations. Should General Roatta adhere to his intention, which he considers tactically absolutely necessary, then Combat Group Bader must also be empowered to negotiate with the national Serbian bands, otherwise the Roatta plan would be endangered. Wehrmacht Commander Southeast requests a decision whether Combat Group Bader may negotiate with national Serbian insurgents according to the directive of the Italian Second Army, should the Roatta plan be adhered to.[21]

In the meantime Combat Group Bader reported that the Croatian government had "proposed" negotiations with the Četniks to the German and Italian offices. However the negotiations must be concluded before the commencement of the operation.[22]

Since it was not possible to synchronize the agreements which had been taken in Abbazia, i.e., Paragraph 10 of the protocol—prohibition of negotiating with the insurgents—with the intention of General Roatta, the OKW through the German General with the Italian Wehrmacht Headquarters in Rome, applied to the Commando Supremo with the request that this contradiction be explained. The OKW deemed it prudent to adhere to the prohibition of negotiations with the insurgents, agreed to in Sušak notwithstanding whether it was a question of Communists or national Serbian bands.[23] The Commando Supremo was also of the same opinion and confirmed through the German General in Rome that he was convinced of the necessity of upholding Paragraph 10 of the protocol of Sušak, and likewise adhered to the prohibition of negotiations with the insurgents. Any deviation whatsoever from the principle could only be effected in complete agreement between the OKW and the Commando Supremo.[24]

Wehrmacht Commander Southeast orders the exploitation of the advance of the Ustasha group

In the area north of the Rogatica-Drina bend as far as Drinjaca-Vlasenica great confusion prevailed among partisan groups of unknown strength and Dangić-Četniks,[25] who were engaged here and there in local fights. On April 8 a fight flared up between Dangić-Četniks and Croatian Ustasha units in Drinjaca. These two Ustasha battalions under Colonel Frantecić had been assigned to block off the northern area near Han Pijesak in the operation against Rogatica. Now, however, these two Ustasha battalions attacked the insurgents from Drinjaca on April 9 and advanced further southwards, took Brotunac on the 10th (Bratunac southeast of Drinjaca) and in a further advance reached Srebrenica on the 11th. On the 11th the Wehrmacht Commander Southeast ordered Combat Group Bader: "If at all possible make use of the advance of Frantecic and in conjunction with the Croatians, clear up the situation in East Bosnia north of the demarcation line before the beginning of the joint operation." Reports confirmed that the insurgents had begun to retreat from the area east of Rogatica towards the south and southeast while still continuing their attack on Rogatica. In the days following the news spread that the Montenegrin bands from the area southwest of Rogatica had also withdrawn to the south and the insurgent groups north of the demarcation line appeared to be growing weaker.

Critical delay of the Italians

In such a situation the news of a delay in the deployment of the Italian fighting forces filled the German command with an understandable displeasure. According to the protocol of Abbazia and also according to the discussions in Laibach the commencement of the operation was intended for April 15. The Italians however were not able to adhere to those agreements. Already on April 9 General Roatta had reported via the German Liaison Officer with the Second Italian Army that the transport of troops to relieve the divisions intended for the operation in Bosnia had been delayed owing to the danger of U-boats. For this reason, and also "because of the deep snow in several regions of north Herzegovina," the operations could not commence before April 25.

In order to free the Italian 22nd Division, "Cacciatori della Alpi," and the 1st Mountain Division "Taurinense" for the operation, the two border divisions, "Emilia" and "Murge," at present in Italy, were made available to the Italian Second Army. At the beginning of April the "Emilia" Division relieves the "Messina" Division at present in the area of Cattaro, the latter to be transferred north into the area previously occupied by the 5th Mountain Division "Pusteria." The transport of the "Murge" Division is delayed owing to limited shipping space and the danger of enemy submarines. The "Murge" Division was to replace the "Cacciatori della Alpi" Division in the area of Dubrovnik, which had to advance into the area of Cacko-Kalinovik. By the delayed arrival of the "Murge" Division, the assembly of the "Cacciatori della Alpi" Division was also delayed. The Division "Taurinense" was being assembled at the beginning of April in order to be dispatched later by rail via Sarajevo into the area Turbe-Trnovo-Trnovo Pass. On April 7 the date for the commencement of the rail transportation was not yet fixed. Five days later, on April 14 General Roatta replied to an enquiry of the German liaison officer, that the transport of the units from Italy was again delayed because of the U-boat danger which still existed, and therefore the "Cacciatori della Alpi" and "Taurinense" divisions could not be ready before April 25.[26] In addition a period of at least 12 days must be reckoned for the transport by rail of the "Taurinense" Division to Sarajevo, since only a few railroad cars are available. Therefore General Bader proposed moving the "Taurinense" Division by foot from its assembly area (Mostar) to Sarajevo along the 80 kilometer approach road, so that it might reach its jumping-off position at the agreed time since rail transport cost too much. The Wehrmacht Commander Southeast and the Italian Second Army seconded this proposal. At the same time General of Artillery Bader had the German liaison officer inform General Roatta of his misgivings regarding another postponement of the operation. He informed General Roatta that preparations until now were probably known to the insurgents, so that the Montenegrin insurgent groups had withdrawn further to the south, unfortunately unhindered by the Italians and had taken all the pillaged cattle and foodstocks with them. Even the remaining insurgents will leave the operational zone. An essential part of the operation, the destruction of the insurgents, had therefore miscarried. The advancing spring season and the trees bursting into leaf precluded a further postponement of the commencement of the operation. Previous operations confirmed, and this had also been discussed in Laibach, that an effective combing of the wooded mountain terrain is only possible before the trees and undergrowth are in leaf. Therefore General Bader insisted with the Italian Second Army that all means be taken for the speedy commencement of the operation.[27] The Wehrmacht Commander Southeast informed the German General in Rome of the proposal of the German liaison officer with the Italian Second Army and asked that a similar strongly emphasized request be made to the Commando Supremo. For the Combat Group Bader had already been ordered on April 11 to exploit the advances of Croatian Lt. Colonel Frantecić in order to prepare the operation.[28]

On April 14 the Wehrmacht Commander Southeast again asked the Combat Group Bader whether an advance of the 118th Infantry Division to the south were possible, or would be possible within a few days. The chief of operations staff of Combat Group Bader advised: "Thrust towards southeast possible, however decison not before April 28 concerning this, according to the situation, as a previous advance would be contrary to Italian orders."

The advance of Lt. Colonel Frantecic' on Vlasnica was carried out contrary to the orders of General Bader, who in addition to General Roatta had expressly forbidden the Ustasha units any independent action whatsoever. Furthermore the advance of the Ustasha on Vlasnica ended in a reverse. The insurgents received support from Serbia through Dangić-Četniks and expelled the Ustasha once more from Srebrenica.

As the German General in Rome reported on the 18th, the Commando Supremo shared misgivings concerning another postponement of the commencement of the operation. He further reported that General Roatta intended to meet General Bader in Bosnia on April 20 and 21, in order to fix with him the time of the commencement of the operation.[29]

Decision to attack Rogatica without waiting for the arrival of the Italians

Despite delays on the part of the Italians and in spite of the presence of the Wehrmacht Commander Southeast, General Bader intended to carry out the operation in East Bosnia according to plan and in accord with the Italian movement. Therefore he had ordered the 718th Infantry Division on April 14 to reach the contemplated encirclement front of Podložnik-Sokolac-Han Pijesak by April 20.

The Ustasha battalions under the command of Lt. Colonel Frantecic' were ordered to reach the Han Pijesak-Podzeplje area by April 20, the III Battalion of the 737th Infantry Regiment with the 714th Engineer Company and were to be subordinated to the 718th Infantry Divsion in place of the tardy Italians. From April 24 the 737th Infantry Regiment was to take over the security of the Drina River from the Zepa estuary as far as Višegrad and to hold one battalion in readiness to be at the disposal of the Commander in Serbia west of Višegrad.

When however the Italians were not able to keep this fixed date, they postponed the beginning of the operation again to the 25th, indicating that they had little desire for action or interest in the military operation. A political aim, the occupation of Sarajevo and East Bosnia, was probably the motive of their tactics.

Conference in Sarajevo

The German generals who met in Headquarters of the Combat Group Bader in Sarajevo on April 19 for a discussion were of this opinion. The following were present: General of Artillery Bader, the German General in Zagreb, General Glaise-Horstenau, the Commander of the 718th Division, General Fortner, the Chief of Staff of the

Combat Group Bader, General Staff Lt. Colonel Pfafferott. On April 20 the following attended the conference: the Croatian representatives, the Chief of Staff in the headquarters of the Poglavnik, General Pribac, the Croatian Foreign Minister Lorkovic, the State Secretary for Police Affairs Kvaternik, the special Plenipotentiary of the Croatian government for East Bosnia for political affairs, Benak and finally the Ustasha Lt. Colonel Frantecić.

At this conference the German General in Zagreb expressed his misgivings that the entry of the Italians into Sarajevo could be disadvantageous to German Balkan policy and to the German policy towards Turkey, especially since religious connections existed between the Moslems of Bosnia, Stambul and Asia Minor. General of Artillery Bader was able to inform the participants at the conference that the order for the mopping up of the area around Rogatica had already been issued. The operation was to begin on the 22nd. General of Artillery Bader stressed a build-up of Croatian administration in the mopped up areas and demanded toleration by the Croatian representatives towards that part of the Serbian population of East Bosnia which was willing to reconstruct. The question of the Ustasha, the stumbling block to pacification was again discussed, and the atrocities exercised by the bands of Hadzi Effendi, armed with Croatian weapons, against the Serbian population of Tuzla and Zvornik were broached. The Croats promised their full support in meeting the German wishes. Above all they desired that the blocking off of the Drina be carried out by the Ustasha battalions of Lt. Colonel Frantecić.

At the conclusion of this conference in Sarajevo, General of Artillery Bader sent a telegram to the Wehrmacht Commander Southeast on April 20 reporting:

"The situation of the Croatian units encircled in Rogatica demands immediate relief. The arrival of the Italian divisions for this purpose [is] further delayed. Nevertheless 718th Infantry Division and Croatian units [are] ready for commitment on April 25. [They are] to fall in from the encirclement front in the area of Praca-Sokolac-Han Pijesak-estuary of the Zepa [two illegible words] on April 22. Time required approximately two weeks. The Italian Second Army is requested to prevent the retreat of the insurgents into the Italian zone of occupation by the commitment of available troops on the demarcation line.[30]

Combat Group Bader suggests that the joint German-Italian operation be called off

In two further telegrams, General of Artillery Bader proposed to the Wehrmacht Commander Southeast that the intended German-

Italian-Croatian operation in East Bosnia be called off with the mopping up of the Rogatica pocket, and the Italians be urged to carry out a thorough mopping up of their own occupation zone for a general pacification of the situation in East Bosnia. An end could then be put to the previous attempts of the Italians to infiltrate into Sarajevo. "Since according to the attitude here," the telegram concluded, "no joint German-Italian operation will be carried out, it is proposed to dissolve the operational staff of the Combat Group Bader at the conclusion of the mopping up of Rogatica and after the building up of the frontier security on the Drina. This task will probably be finished on May 15."[31] And finally in the evening of April 20 General of Artillery Bader reported: "Joint German-Italian operation miscarried due to absence of Italians. Mopping up of the Rogatica pocket continues. A subsequent fitting in of Italian forces no longer possible because fanning out displacements are impossible in the mountainous terrain.

"In the present situation "Trio II" (Drina bend) and "Trio III" (Ozren) are no longer necessary. After the sealing off of the Drina frontier and mopping up of both Drina bends ("Trio I" continues, "Trio II" carried out by the Frantecić advance) an overall clearing up seems probable. The reformation of the Croatian government contributed considerably towards this as far as Serbia was concerned.

"Therefore there is no longer any necessity for the commitment of Italian forces in the German occupation zone. Proposal: cessation of transport to Sarajevo, commitment of Italian troops in Sarajevo for mopping up south of Sarajevo and for the return march to be effected with the OKW."[32]

On May 28 the previously existing Combat Group Bader was dissolved, and the elements of the 521st Signals Regiment as well as the 659th Engineer Battalion which had been with it, were transferred to the West Bosnian Combat Group.

In the meantime, on May 23 and 25, the Commanding General and Commander in Serbia had issued to the newly formed West Bosnian Combat Group basic orders for the new operation.[33] Marshal Kvaternik had agreed to German High Command control over all Croatian units to be committed in the West Bosnian operation and also declared himself in agreement with the day fixed for the beginning of the operation, June 15. In all, the Croats wanted to make available three mountain divisions with about 11 battalions. In addition there were the Croatian units already committed for the sealing off of the insurgent territory.[34] West Bosnia was declared an operational zone by the Croatian government and executive authority was transferred to the Brigadier General and Commander in Serbia.

The West Bosnian Operation

By the beginning of June the situation in West Bosnia yielded the following picture: according to Croatian reports six to seven thousand men, well armed and well organized bands occupied the territory Bos. Gradiska-Sava-Una-Kostajnica-Bos. Novi-Prijedor-west of Banja Luka.

The main insurgent center was apparently in the wild rugged wooded mountains of the Kozara range. Croatian security was at the moment in the east of the insurgent territory in the line Bos. Gradiska to west of Banja Luka, then in the south in and around Sanski Most, in the west on the Una from Bos. Novi as far as the confluence of the Una and the Sava. Between Banja Luka and the Croatian group in Sanski Most as well as between Kostajnica and Bos. Novi there was no Croatian security. The bridgeheads of Bos. Dubica-Kostajnica-Dobrlin and Bos. Novi were in the possession of the Croats. To the north of the insurgent territory the Sava plain was inundated, in parts up to a width of 8 kilometers. Some of the Croatian mountain brigades had already arrived. Others were being disembarked, the 1st and the 2nd in the area of Bos. Novi-Kostajnica, the 3rd near Banja Luka.

Croatian reverses

In the meantime on the 15th the Croatian Group west of Banja Luka had retreated before an attempt of the insurgents to break out; however by the commitment of reserves a break through of the insurgents encircled in the Kozara Mountains was prevented. In the following days renewed local efforts of the enemy bands to break through on the southern blockade line were also repulsed.

However, the Croatian 1st Mountain Division suffered a severe reverse. The 2nd Mountain Brigade, committed on its left flank retreated on the 19th before superior enemy pressure once more to the west across the Prijedor-Bos. Dubica highway. With the help of German forces this Croatian brigade was able to take up its old position. Only the Combat Group West Bosnia which on the 20th went in to attack against the wooded, rugged Kozara Mountains, came up in the south and southwest against a tenacious and well armed adversary who knew how to defend himself cleverly in his mountain positions on the edges of crags and defiles and frequently went over to counter-attacks. Even women took part in the fight. When the 1st Croatian Mountain Division, carelessly and unprepared, collided with this strong enemy on the western edge of the Kozara, its front crumbled. On the 21st the 2nd Croatian Brigade suffered another heavy reverse. On the next day, the 22nd, the insurgents advanced against the northern flank of the Croatians and threw back the 1st Croatian Mountain Brigade too across the Bos. Dubica-Prijedor highway as far as ten kilometers southwest of Bos. Dubica. Seized by panic the Croatians streamed back before this surprise counterattack of the enemy. Two Croatian battalions lost all their ammunition, all their machine guns and their whole equipment.

In the period from July 18-25 the 1st and 2nd Croatian Mountain Brigades lost 235 dead, 182 wounded, 521 missing, 108 horses, 53 light machine guns, 15 heavy machine guns, 15 mortars and three mountain guns.

In these critical days Brigadier General Stahl, the Commander of the West Bosnian Combat Group intervened to aid the unsteady Croats. He was concerned with closing the break which had occurred southwest of Bos. Dubica in order to prevent the insurgents breaking out into the Kozara Mountains.

On June 23, the enemy who had already advanced across the Una, was thrown back once more everywhere across the Prijedor-Bos. Dubica highway and the situation was once more restored. The 2nd Croatian Brigade supported by German forces now held the sector Prijedor-Muratti, and the 1st Brigade held the high ridges east of the Muratti-Bos. Dubica highway.[35]

Further attempts of the enemy to break out in these positions on the western edge of the Kozara were prevented with the aid of the weak German units quickly placed in front of the 1st Croatian Mountain Division. Only with the severest attack and only after the commitment of all the available forces was it possible to again build up this front on the Prijedor-Bos. Dubica line. The Croatian brigades which had suffered so badly seemed hardly capable of carrying on the attack. Therefore Brigadier General Stahl intended to concentrate all available troops around the southern group in order to continue temporarily with this group the attack against the insurgents in the Kozara, while the 1st Croatian Mountain Brigade reinforced by German battalions had to first seal off the mountain terrain in the west.

In these critical days it appeared that the surprising capture of Prijedor and Ljubia on the 10th and 11th of June by our troops, had after the first shock, only induced the insurgents encircled in the Kozara to increasing activity. Other insurgent groups from the south, out of the Italian zone of occupation moved over the demarcation line into the rear of the encircling front of the West Bosnian Combat Group.

Evacuation of the Italians from the 3rd Zone of Occupation and the consequences thereof

Towards the end of May the Wehrmacht Commander Southeast estimated that the Montenegrin Proletarian brigades retreating from the area of Rogatica towards the south did not at the moment threaten to return to German occupied territory. The return of these Montenegrin insurgent groups to East Bosnia seemed improbable, especially since the intention of General Roatta of leaving the "Taurinense" and "Pustoria" divisions for the time being in their present operational area (territory around Mostar, Cacko, Foca Kalinovik) was known to the Wehrmacht Commander Southeast. Even an invasion towards southwest Serbia did not seem probable at the moment since according to experience the Montenegrins feared the German units. Liaison between the Montenegrin insurgents and the rest of the Mihailovic´ bands also seemed improbable since Mihailovic´, at least up until now, had never made common cause with the Communists. However at the moment there were no facts present to warrant such a conclusion.

The Wehrmacht Commander Southeast presumed rather that the Montenegrin bands intended to make contact with the landing bases of the enemy U-boats in the area of Cattoro-Ragusa and for this purpose create a continuous insurgent area in the Italian zone.

The Wehrmacht Commander Southeast believed it possible to carry out the pacification of Serbia and Croatia with the forces at present available together with the newly set up SS division "Prinz Eugen," however he requested the OKW to refrain from another withdrawal of troops from the southeast area, otherwise help through an exchange of forces between the north and south Balkans, which was necessary for the pacification, and the continuation of the reinforcement of Crete could not be carried out.[36]

However, soon after the joint German-Italian mopping up of Foča, the Italians changed their intentions and task measures which led to an influx of insurgents from northwest Montenegro into the area southwest of the demarcation line and thereby to a new and unexpected threat from the south to the German occupation zone.

Already at the beginning of the mopping up operation the Italians had withdrawn their units south of the demarcation zone from the Herzegovinian-Bosnian-Dalmatian mountains into the vicinity of the Adriatic coast. They started these movements already July 11, but waiting until four days later to inform German headquarters of these important measures. By the evacuation of a large part of the third zone along the demarcation line, and of parts of the second zone adjoining it to the south, the situation had fundamentally changed.

The insurgents could now assemble unhindered on and south of the demarcation line, especially since sufficient Croatian occupation troops were lacking in the areas denuded of Italian units, and from there could continually threaten the German occupation zone and make completely impossible the pacification of the young Croatian state.

Through the Chief of the General Staff, General Foertsch, the Wehrmacht Commander Southeast expressly called the attention of the OKW, on June 22, to these dangers which had arisen through the evacuation of the Italians.*

On July 2 the Wehrmacht Commander Southeast again remonstrated to the OKW on account of the evacuation of the territory south and west of the German-Italian demarcation line by the Italian Second Army. The pacification of the evacuated areas was in the future to be left exclusively to Croatian units. For this supposed pacification in their own zone of occupation the Italians made extensive use of national Serbian bands. With the arrival of new Croatian units, the Wehrmacht Commander Southeast reported to the OKW, clashes between the National Serbians and the Croatians are unavoidable. The Croatian units are equal neither to the National Serbians nor to the Communists. Hence the area evacuated by the Italians must become a continuous insurgent center. Therefore German interests are also endangered. An encroachment of the unrest into the German occupation zone would make difficult the pacification of the areas around Prijedor and Sarajevo, which were so important to the war economy. After the suppression of the insurgents in West Bosnia, the Wehrmacht Commander Southeast would endeavor to prevent an encroachment of the insurgents from the Italian zone into the German occupation zone.

The Wehrmacht Commander Southeast proposed that the OKW request the Commando Supremo that the Italian area of occupation around Mostar be extended and secured so that the bauxite mines there and the transport of the ore from the Italian occupation zone remain guaranteed.[37]

Mopping up of the Kozara Mountains

In the meantime, after June 26 German reinforcements from Bosnia had arrived in Bos. Dubica. The west group front was once more strengthened by the German reinforcements which were sent in. At the beginning of July preparations for the continuation of the attack against the Kozara Mountains were concluded.

---

* Just at this critical time General Foertsch had gone to a conference with OKW.

On July 5, the West Bosnian Combat Group, reinforced by forces from Serbia, fell in again from the south and west for the attack on the Kozara Mountains. Just before the attack, renewed attempts of the insurgents to break out on the Una had led to local penetrations of the Croatian forces. However the insurgents were thrown back with bloody losses and the situation between Bos. Novi and Kostajnica was once more restored. The insurgents then retreated to the northwest before the concentrated attack of the West Bosnian Combat Group. On the 5th approximately 1,800 insurgent deserters and refugees, among them two-thirds women and children, were reported on the eastern blockade line.

In the days following (July 6-12) the attack in the Kozara Mountains made good progress. The insurgents withdrew fighting. Croatian units and our own patrolled the densely wooded mountain terrain which was thoroughly combed and mopped up. In collaboration with the Hungarian Danube flotilla a German tank platoon broke up band concentrations in the Sava valley and prevented an enemy attempt to cross the river. Wherever the insurgents tried to break through the encirclement, in the northwest, in the west, and in the southwest, they were thrown back with bloody losses.[38]

On July 8 the southern main ridge of the Kozara mountain range was in our hands. From approximately the 10th onwards only local resistance was still present.

The bandits buried their weapons and left their hiding places. On the eastern blockade line the stream of refugees increased to thousands, altogether 7,790 deserters and refugees were reported there.

On July 13 our troops approached from the south and west patrolling the thickly wooded terrain of the Prozora, the northern foothills of the Kozara mountain range. During the continuing mopping up, operation weapons —2.15 cm gun barrels, explosives, equipment of all kinds and propaganda material—were captured and more than 100 horses and herds of cattle were brought into the collecting camps.

Mopping up of the Prozora

On July 13 our units concluded their regrouping for the attack against band remnants encircled in the Prozora east of Bos. Dubica. On the 14th in heavy rain and under great difficulties as far as terrain was concerned, the operation commenced. The advance was carried out sector by sector and with a thorough mopping up. On the 15th the main ridge of the thickly wooded Prozora was reached. Attempts to break out by the encircled bands were in vain. On the next day on the 16th the east and west attacking flanks arrived in the Sava plain northeast of Bos. Dubica. Fleeing band remnants which tried to escape across the Sava were destroyed. On the 17th the last enemy resistance in the Sava plain was speedily broken up by the continuation of the attack north of the Prozora. The band remnants—300 strong—surrendered their weapons.

With this the operation in the Kozara and the Prozora mountains was concluded on July 18 with great success. From July 9-23 the West Bosnian Combat Group suffered the following losses: *German*: dead 33, wounded 80, missing 10; *Croats*: dead 135, wounded 54, missing 7; *insurgents*: dead 1,626, wounded 273, prisoners 8,849, shot in reprisal 431.

Combat directives of the Wehrmacht Commander Southeast

The influx of the insurgents into the areas evacuated by the Italians resulted in the focal point of the combatting of the bands continuing to occur in Croatia. This was expressed in a directive for the conduct of the war in Croatia which was issued on July 12 by the Wehrmacht Commander Southeast.

". . . the operation in West Bosnia has led to the desired results, the destruction of the continuous insurgent area between the Sava-Una-Sana-Urivaja-Vrbas.

"Nevertheless a new situation which affects the whole of Croatia has arisen through the rapid evacuation of nearly all of Zone 3 and parts of Zone 2 by Italian troops, permitting complete freedom of movement to the insurgents in these areas. The transfer of weak Croatian occupation units to these areas would not be an effective counter-measure.

"The insurgents endeavored to advance to the north and northwest from the area south of Bos. Novi, Sanski Most, south of Jajce and southwest and south of Sarajevo, to bring relief to the bands encircled in the Kozara. Probably, however, the intention is to acquire the Samarica Mountains starting from the Grna Mountains, and from there, the area around Petrinja as a continuous insurgent territory. Thereby the insurgents would have threatened the Sava valley and the area around Zagreb in which all communications vital for German and Croatian interest alike converge.

"With the spread of band activity north of the Sava increasingly evident commitments of the majority of the Italian forces in northwest Croatia, Dalmatia and Slovenia, and of the other elements on the Adriatic coast, indicates that except in the area around Karlovac, no further collaboration between German, Italian and Croatian troops can be reckoned with in the future.

"The Mihailović organization is spreading from southern Serbia to Montenegro and Bosnia, possibly also to Slovenia and Croatia north of the Sava. Even if the Mihailović organization cannot yet be regarded as ready to attack, time and further development could lead to a unified command of all band groups by Mihailović. In this respect the differences between Mihailović and the Communist leaders may not be regarded as insurmountable. Suitable orders are said to have been issued from London and Moscow."

The Wehrmacht Commander Southeast estimated that the revolutionary and organizational activity of Mihailović would spread to all of Serbia. Therefore the task of the Commanding General and Commander in Serbia remains unchanged for Serbia and Croatia: security of communications important for operational purposes, and safeguarding and exploitation of plants and industrial centers important to the German war economy. The Wehrmacht Commander Southeast gave the following directives for the conduct of the war:

In Serbia the present pacification is to be maintained by mobile reserves. The most dangerous opponent is Mihailović; his organization must not be allowed to become effective; a joining up of the bands was to be prevented by operations. Any revolt which might flare up had to be nipped in the bud by attack. In view of the development of the situation in North Africa particular stress was laid upon the security of the operationally important Semlin-Saloniki railroad.

In Croatia it was most important to prevent the formation of another contiguous insurgent territory directly after the conclusion of the operation in West Bosnia. The acquired territories were to be pacified as in East Bosnia. The influx of insurgents from the Italian zone was to be hindered by the occupation and prior setting up of support points at the crossing south of Bos. Novi, Sanski Most, Banja Luka (V. Vakuf, Jajce, D. Vakuf) southwest and southeast of Sarajevo, and thereby at the same time guarantee reconnaissance activity into the Italian territtory, and secure communication with the Croatian garrison in Zone 3.

By means of a mobile conduct of the war the joining up of the bands in the other German-occupied areas of Croatia, as well as north of the Sava, was also to be prevented. Therefore the mountains directly north of the Zagreb-Belgrade railroad were to be mopped up first if possible. The protection of the Reich border-Semlin railroad was to be reinforced by three security groups. The creation of two adjoining zones of occupation, between the Bosna and Vrbas rivers, with occupation groups and at least one combined reinforced Croatian division and reinforced Croatian units, is to be aimed at.[39]

The operation in the Samarica

Scarcely was the mopping up completed in the Una-Sana bend, when at the beginning of August a new operation began: the mopping up of the mountain territory of the Samarica, lying west of the Kostajnica-Bos. Novi line. Already in the middle of July the Commanding General and Commander in Serbia had laid the plans for the destruction of the insurgents in the Samarica. According to these the Kostajnica-Bos. Novi line was to be sealed off and the enemy in the Samarica was to be destroyed and dispersed by an advance from the northeast to the southwest.[40]

The enemy in the Samarica totalling about 1,400 armed men, terrorized and partly controlled Petrinja-Glina-Otoka-west of Bos. Novi-Blinja and even encroached on the northern bank of the Sava. In the region of Otoka the enemy was in uninterrupted communication with the insurgents in the Grmec Mountains, and south of Klina with those in the Petrova Gora.

The Commander of the West Bosnian Combat Group was of the opinion that in consideration of the size of the insurgent territory, and with the smaller number of troops available, the bands in the Samarica could not be first encircled and sealed off from all sides, before they were destroyed, as had happened to the guerrillas in the Kozara. To prevent the insurgents in the Grmec Mountains from supporting and reinforcing the rebels in the Samarica, the Una between Bos. Novi and Otoka must be sealed off and occupied. In order to encircle all the insurgents the area south of the Bos. Novi-Glina highway as far as the Ozoka-Topuska highway must be seized. During the mopping up of this area the blockade line on the Bos. Novi-Glina highway was threatened from the south by the insurgents in the Grmec Mountains and in the Petrova Gora. An encirclement front, 150-200 kilometers long, as the crow flies, would have had to be built around the area of Samarica.

In the most propitious circumstances, only the 721st Infantry Regiment, with two battalions, approximately 1,100 men, the 734th Infantry Regiment, four to five batteries, the 202nd Panzer Battalion with two companies, the 659th Engineer Battalion with two companies, 300 men—and of Croatian units the 1st Mountain Division with the 1st and 2nd Mountain Brigades, approximately 4,500 rifles, forces of the Blockade Group West, 1,500 men, about four battalions of the Croatian Infantry Corps Sisak, 2,000 men, were available for the creation of an encirclement front. Each battalion with 500 rifles must be allotted a sector 7.5 to 10 kilometers wide in order to be able to create an encirclement front.

In contrast to the insurgents in the Kozara, those in the Samarica were neither static nor associated with the population, which only to a small extent had any connections with the Communist insurgents who came from other territories. To seize all men above the age of 14, as in the Kozara, was not possible, for the necessary forces were lacking and such an action would also have driven the majority of the population of the Samarica over to the Communist insurgents.

The Commander of the West Bosnian Combat Group also believed that after the formation and narrowing of the encirclement front, the mopping up of the actual Samarica—a much intersected, inaccessible area, covered partly with forest and thick undergrowth, with few roads and little water, would provide such terrain difficulties for troops not suitably equipped, that the expected success would in no way materialize.

The Commander of the West Bosnian Combat Group reckoned that a period of at least four weeks would be necessary for the operation in the Samarica. However after the conclusion of the mopping up of the Una-Sana bend, the 1st Croatian Mountain Division was urgently in need of rest as it had been committed without a break since the end of March. The operation would cause great difficulties for the Croatian government as far as men, material, clothing and equipment for these severely tested divisions were concerned. The employment of the majority of the units of the West Bosnian Combat Group for at least a month, could not be defended, since reserves were to be held free for a possible operation in a southern direction, and because of the critical situation north of the Sava, mopping up operations were necessary in the Psunje Mountains and in the Fruska Gora.

As a result of all these considerations, the Commander of the West Bosnian Combat Group proposed to occupy the Samarica, and the previous insurgent villages in this area, holding occasional strong points with one battalion from which the enemy was to be dispersed and destroyed by continuous small scale operations. For the carrying out of these tasks, German motorized units (202nd Panzer Battalion, elements of the 659th Engineer Battalion, 659th Infantry Company in trucks), as well as the 1st Croatian Mountain Division and forces of the I Croatian Corps Sisak, and of these forces a few Croatian battalions were to be left for the security of the mopped up area, after the destruction of the majority of the guerrillas.

The 3rd Croatian Mountain Brigade was first to remain committed against the Grmec Mountains, whilst the 721st Infantry Regiment

(less one battalion in the area of Prijedor and Ljubia) and forces of
the 704th Infantry Division which became free, and the newly set
up 4th Croatian Mountain Brigade could then be committed for
mopping up in Slavonia (Psunje or Syrmia).[41]

On August 8 the German-Croatian West Bosnian Combat Group
fell in for the mopping up of the Samarica mountain range. The advance from the north through the mountains to the south was un-
eventful. The enemy retreated from the mountains toward the west
over the demarcation line. After a few hundred insurgents had been
taken prisoner the mopping up of the Samarica mountain range was
concluded around August 20.

The total losses in Croatia in the period from August 9 to 24
amounted to:

German		*Croatian*	
Dead	2	Dead	77
Wounded	12	Wounded	108
Missing	1	Missing	362

Insurgent	
Dead	1,031
Wounded	273
Prisoners	260
Shot in reprisal	212

Mopping up of the Psunj Mountains

The Communist bands situated north of the Sava—the order read
for Psunj operation—have up until now organized themselves almost
undisturbed, and undertaken ever-increasing attacks and raids on
railroads and gendarmerie stations. The population is being terrorized. The Volksdeutsche are being persecuted and in many cases
murdered, the harvest is being destroyed and carried away.

Together with the continuation of its present tasks the West Bosnian Combat Group will mop up the Psunj mountain area-Pakrad-
Banevo Jaruga-Bos. Gradiška, and will destroy the insurgents there.

Mopping up of the Fruška Gora

Only four days after the conclusion of the operation in the Psunj
Mountains, a new operation commenced, the mopping up of the
Fruška Gora area. From the east and from the west a German battalion advanced by surprise through the Fruška Gora region, while the
Hungarian Danube Flotilla fought enemy concentrations on the
northern edge of the mountain range. The operation went according
to plan, with occasional strong enemy resistance and was concluded

on September 1. The insurgents had been successfully taken by surprise in the Fruška Gora and a great success had been achieved. Altogether the enemy lost 353 dead and 1,032 prisoners in this operation.

The West Bosnian Combat Group was dissolved on August 29. Its losses from the beginning of the operation (June 10) amounted to:

Germans: dead   71
        wounded 187
        missing   8
Croats: dead   475
        wounded 727
        missing   510
*Insurgents:*dead   4,735
        prisoners 12,207

Losses in the territory of the command of the Commanding General and Commander in Serbia (Serbia and Croatia) for the period August 9-24, 1942:

Germans: dead   2
        wounded   1
Croatians: dead   77
        wounded 108
        missing   162
*Insurgents:*dead   1,031
        wounded 273
        prisoners 2,168
        shot in
         reprisal 212

Combats on the German-Italian demarcation line

While these combats were being carried out bands which had appeared in East Bosnia were broken up by successful small scale mopping up operations of the 718th Infantry Division near Zavidovica, near Tuzla, in the Drina bend near Vlasenica and near Rogatica. At the beginning of July our units had to ward off a penetration of insurgents from the Italian occupation zone in the area south and west of Sarajevo. The enemy lost more than 100 dead. A strong insurgent group which advanced at the end of July from the Italian occupation zone across the demarcation line into the area of Sarajevo was encircled by units of the 718th Infantry Division and completely destroyed. The enemy lost 500 dead and numerous wounded.

During August the unrest in the Italian zone of occupation increased and became stronger around the middle of the month. The Wehrmacht Commander Southeast stressed continually with the

OKW to remonstrate with the Commando Supremo that at least the supervision of the railroads and highways in the third zone as far as the demarcation line be taken over again by the Italians in order to protect the ore territory which was vital for the war armament and to guarantee the transport of the ore which had been mined. Without sufficient protection it was to be feared that the personnel of the bauxite mines in Mostar would go over to the side of the Communist insurgents.[42]

When in the middle of August the situation in the bauxite area in Mostar became more critical, and the insurgents from the area Goražde-Foča once more advanced against the German occupation zone in the north, the Italians in the evacuated zone pulled themselves together for a mopping up operation. On the 26th they reoccupied Foča, after the insurgents had withdrawn from this locality. In the bauxite area of Mostar the situation was again quiet.

Combats which flared up frequently with the bands that had forced their way into the area south of Banja Luka towards Bugojno, D. Vakuf, Jajce, V. Vakuf, and Sanski Most from northwest Herzegovina characterized the situation. Around August 18 a band effected an incursion near Sanski Most and attacked the Croatian garrison there. The Jajce-Bogojno railroad was continually interrupted by explosions. Insurgents from the area of the Grmec Mountains also advanced against Bos. Novi and endangered once more the ore mines near Prijedor. Elements of the 1st Croatian Mountain Division broke up bands which had advanced into the area west of Bos. Novi. In August there was a clash on the demarcation line southwest of Banja Luka between a Croatian battalion and insurgents. An insurgent group surprised the Croatian garrison in V. Vakuf—350 Croatians surrendered their arms. In the meantime a German battalion from Banja Luka was committed. On the 26th it contacted southwest of this place a strong enemy armed with infantry guns, anti-tank guns, anti-aircraft guns and mortars. One tank was put out of action. Two Croatian aircraft were shot down. While the German battalion fought in the last days of August against bands which had advanced over the demarcation line towards Banja Luka, approximately 2,000 Serbian Nationalists joined the German units to ward off the Communist bands. The enemy was thrown back out of the German zone of occupation towards the south and west.

The Situation in Serbia

In Serbia since the beginning of 1942 it had been generally quiet with the exception of local unrest, isolated surprise attacks and sabotage acts. By the concentration of all available forces (Russian factory guards, Serbian State Guards, and volunteer units) small sized bands had been successfully fought by our occupation divisions. The 7th Company of the 800 Brandenburg Instruction Regiment for special employment distinguished itself both in Serbia and in the Fruska Gora. At the beginning of July this company had to be handed over to the Eastern front.

In the Bulgarian zone of occupation small size mopping up operations were successfully carried out with the cooperation of the 717th Infantry Division in the area southeast of Niš, south of Prokuplje, in Jastrebac and finally at the beginning of August also in the Kopaonik Mountains.

The railroad lines Zagreb-Belgrad-Sofia and Salonika as well as the Danube were guarded for the current traffic by the commitment of German and Bulgarian units as well as the German and Royal Hungarian Danube flotillas. Production in the copper, lead and antimony works which was especially important to the German war industry was able to continue undisturbed under German protection.

Altogether the number of those shot in battle or as reprisal amounted in the first year of combatting of the insurgent movement in Serbia and Croatia to: 49,724. During the month of August the whole 714th Infantry Division was transferred from Serbia to West Bosnia, the 718th Infantry Division continued to devote itself to its security tasks in East Bosnia. Both divisions were also assigned to the protection of the vital Reich's border-Zagreb-Belgrade railroad. Three regional defense battalions were available as mobile reserve and a temporarily formed motorized infantry battalion under the command of the railroad security staff. In Serbia the zone of occupation of the Bulgarian Occupation Corps and of the 704th Infantry Division remained unchanged. At the beginning of September the 717th Infantry Divsion was transferred into northwest Serbia into the former area of the 714th Infantry Division, and the SS Division "Prinz Eugen" which had been newly set up in the Banat was transferred to southwest Serbia into the area of the 717th Infantry Division. Panzer companies stood in readiness as mobile reserves.

On August 8, the former chief of Luftflotte 4, Generaloberst Loehr, took over the command in the southeast area as Wehrmacht Commander Southeast and Commander in Chief of the 12th Army in place of General of Engineers Kuntze who had been recalled for another assignment.[43]

CONCLUSION

By early 1943 the anti-guerrilla front of Germany, Italy and the Ustasha government in Zagreb had begun to crack at the seams and was breaking down. With the collapse of Italy six months later and the prospects for an Allied victory greatly enhanced, Germany's fortunes in the southeastern conflict began to ebb.

If one accepts the premise that the resistance movement was, in the main, a national reaction against the occupier with important social impulses, then the outbreak of guerrilla warfare was foreordained from the moment the Axis powers carved up and occupied Yugoslavia in 1941. The Ustasha excesses frequently blamed for the outbreak of the revolt in the Independent Croatian State were probably more contributory feeders of the uprising than seminal cause, particularly in the areas outside Croatia where the Ustasha were not present and fratricidal conflict did not take place. The revolts that swept through Serbia, Montenegro and Macedonia were directed against the occupation, tapping important wellsprings of national tradition in the process.

From the fall of Yugoslavia the Germans were saddled with the Ustasha regime which the pro-Ustasha and fanatic Nazi consul in Zagreb, Siegfried Kasche, pointedly reminded Berlin was their only ally in the south Slav area in the fight against the guerrillas. This premise was accepted by Hitler and the OKW head General Keitel in rejecting Italian General Roatta's suggestion of a modus vivendi arrangement with the Orthodox population and by implication the elimination of the Ustasha regime. Keitel's statement is worth requoting here in order to comprehend German thinking.

> In my opinion the prerequisites for arriving at an amicable agreement with the insurgents do not exist. The continuation of the present uncertain situation prevents any conciliation of the Croatian state and in the long run must lead to its dissolution.
>
> Passive endurance of the intrigues of the Panslavs, Četniks, and Communists strengthens these forces in view of the limited powers of the Croatian government and can suddenly become a danger to the whole Balkan situation. Therefore, everything must be accomplished both militarily and politically in order to strengthen the Croatian government to support energetically its measures against the insurgents and to help it in the building up of its power.

Thus, Keitel and probably Hitler believed the Ustasha regime to be the linchpin of Germany's position in the southeast whose demise would immediately be followed by chaos in that region.

Even if the Germans had arrived at an accommodation with the Orthodox population in the western regions it is doubtful if the situation would have changed. Whether the Ustasha regime was replaced by a more tractable Croatian government or military rule, the Axis powers would still have been present on Yugoslav soil as occupiers and the raison d'etre of the guerrilla movement would have continued to exist. After 1942 and the increasing certitude of a final Allied victory, it was even more unlikely that the revolt would abate. For all these reasons the Germans continued to support the Ustasha regime. However, since this was politically unacceptable to the Italians, the two Axis powers were constantly in conflict with one another. The failure to overcome these differences spelled the inability to consolidate the anti-guerrilla front.

Another serious handicap was the low priority assigned to the war in the southeast by the German High Command. Increasingly hard-pressed on the Russian and western fronts as the war progressed, the OKW was extremely reluctant to transfer front line troops and equipment to stamp out the fire in the rear areas. Except for short term commitments of forces when major campaigns were being mounted or when emergency situations necessitated the immediate transference of major support such as the transference of two divisions to wipe out the threatening revolt in Western Serbia in 1941, generally a make-do attitude was adopted toward the southeastern theater. German forces there had to overcome their deficiencies by more effective organization and planning. To make matters worse, replacement forces sent to the Balkans were often over-age men; oftentimes the German occupation forces had too little equipment and armament, much of which came from the plundered stocks of the French, Belgian and other campaigns. Hence, the Germans sought to destroy a dynamic and mobile foe by an essentially holding action strategy.

An additional problem was the conflict between the operational combat forces responsible to the Oberkommando des Wehrmacht and the territorial units of the occupation administration responsible to the Oberkommando des Heeres. The static nature of the occupation units with their defensive strategy attachment to territorial areas clashed with the operational combat units. The latter tended to be more ruthless and willing to use methods of force and terror against the population than the occupation administration based in the area. With the transference of authority in the southeast from the OKH to the OKW the authority of the occupational administration in the area diminished considerably.

In this connection, the German occupation administration was anything but well-coordinated and smooth functioning, resembling more individual fiefs presided over by petty bureaucrats jealous of their power. The authority and jurisdiction of the military leaders conflicted with the functions of the Nazi Party officials who were appointed by the different Nazi Party agencies in Berlin and responsible to them only. At times they overruled the regional commanders. In Serbia, for example, the SS Police officials had more power in some areas than the military commander and administration heads and were responsible only to Himmler. Similarly, the Plenipotentiary for the Economy in Serbia, Neuhaussen, a rather corrupt Nazi official, was a favorite of Goering's and reported only to him. Frequently, needless to say, these officials got into one another's hair and their quarrels had to be referred to Berlin for decision. In Croatia, the Nazi Party Foreign Office representative, Kasche, was generally at odds with the military commander in Croatia, von Glaise Horstenau. These jurisdictional conflicts and feuds were ended only by the appointment of an overall political representative in the southeast, the Foreign Office official Neubacher, whose jurisdiction did not, however, extend to Croatia.

The political myopia and inflexibility of Hitler and the OKW in Berlin also created obstacles for the field commanders in combatting the guerrillas. One of the gravest errors directly traceable to Hitler and the OKW in Berlin was the policy of taking and executing hostages in reprisal for attacks on German personnel to dissuade the population from aiding the guerrillas. A high level of such reprisal executions would also persuade the guerrillas that such attacks would be too costly in human lives. However, the policy of terror only succeeded in arousing a people already harboring feelings of humiliation and resentment against the conquerors and in filling the guerrilla armies. The sight of one's countrymen hanging from lampposts and gibbets does not generally inspire feelings of endearment toward the foreign occupiers. This policy was suspended only in 1944 at the eleventh hour when the worst SS Police chiefs were recalled and the area commanders simply evaded or ignored execution orders—but by then it was too late. The damage had already been done.

Guerrilla wars, the historical record shows, are extremely difficult to quash—even under the most favorable circumstances. Among the most important requisites for effectively combatting a guerrilla insurrection, if we may be permitted to abstract from the lessons of the guerrilla war in southeastern Europe, are unity of effort and purpose, abundant supplies, well trained men, arms and equipment, the sophisticated treatment of the population so as to isolate the guerrillas from their support bases, and a well-coordinated leadership conducting an equally well-coordinated, carefully developed political and military strategy. Though they fought well against their guerrilla adversaries, the Germans unfortunately lacked many of these requirements; the results might have been different otherwise.

NOTES

INTRODUCTION

1. Historical literature on the war is growing. A number of book-length studies have been published on the subject. On the četniks the most recent are Jozo Tomasevich, *The Chetniks* (Stanford 1975) and Matteo J. Milazzo, *The Chetnik Movement and the Yugoslav Resistance* (Baltimore, 1975). An attempt to analyze the struggle without the aid of the major archival sources is Walter R. Roberts, *Tito, Mihailović and the Allies, 1941-1945* (New Brunswick, N.J., 1973). On the wartime Ustasha State a Hungarian journalist and German historian have produced an excellent study: Ladislaus Hory and Martin Broszat, *Der kroatische Ustascha Staat 1941-1945* (Stuttgart, 1965). For a study by an adherent of the rightist Zbor movement see Borivoje M. Karapandžić, *Gradjanski rat u srbiji 1941-1945* (Civil War in Serbia 1941-1945) (Cleveland, 1958). A study by a relative of the wartime Serbian leader, Milan Nedić, is Stanislav Krakov, *General Milan Nedić, na ostrici noža* (General Milan Nedić, On the Razor's Edge)(Munich, 1963). A survey of the war from the partisan side is Ahmet Djonlagić, *Yugoslavia in the Second World War* (Belgrade, 1967). A recent valuable addition by a leader of the partisans is Milovan Djilas, *Wartime* (N.Y., 1977). See also Phyllis Auty, *British Policy Towards Wartime Resistance in Yugoslavia and Greece* (London, 1975). A Yugoslav study based primarily upon Yugoslav archival material is Dušan Penca, *Medjunarodni odnosi jugoslavije u toku drugog svjetskog rata* (The International Relations of Yugoslavia during the Second World War)(Belgrade, 1962). An important eyewitness account is Vladimir Dedijer, *Dnevnik* (Diary), 4 vols., (Belgrade, 1945). The Yugoslav government has also published a massive account of the war by the Vojnoistoriski Institut JNA, *Zbornik dokumenata i podataka o narodno-oslobodilačkom ratu jugoslovenskih naroda* (Military-Historical Institute, Collection of Documents and Facts about the National Liberation Struggle of the Yugoslav Peoples). See also my own survey of the war, Paul N. Hehn, "Serbia, Croatia and Germany 1941-1945: Civil War and Revolution in the Balkans," *Canadian Slavonic Papers*, 1969, pp. 344-373.

2. Nedić's meeting with Hitler is described in the memoirs of the wartime German political chief in the southeast, Hermann Neubacher, *Sonderauftrag Südost, 1940-1945: Bericht eines fliegenden Diplomaten* (Gottingen, 1956), pp. 134ff.

3. *Unpublished German Documents of WW II*, Agram, (Zagreb), October 1, 1941, Glaise to OKW, German General in Agram File 309/41 (hereafter GGAF); Agram, October 3, 1941, 312/41; Agram, December 30, 1941, Glaise to OKW, GGAF 431/41.

4. Lothar Rendulic, *Gekampft gesiegt, geschlagen* (Wells, 1952), p. 210.

5. *German Anti-Guerrilla Operations in the Balkans* (1941-1944), Dept. of the Army, 1954, Pamphlet No. 30-243, p. 11.

6. Discussions on the guerilla movement in the southeast in December 1942 and again in 1943 are described in F. W. Deakin, *The Brutal Friendship* (London, 1962), pp. 134 55 and 183-200.

7. *German Anti-Guerrilla Operations in the Balkans*, p. 46.

8. For a good analysis of the 1941 uprising in Montenegro see Djilas, *Wartime*, pp. 16ff.

9. The conflict in western Serbia is described in *The Trial of Dragoljub-Draza Mihailović* (Belgrade, 1946), pp. 409-17; Karapandžić, *Gradjanski rat u srbiji*, pp. 105-107, pp. 118-22; Jovan Marjanović, *Ustanak i narodnoslobodilački pokret u srbiji 1941* (The Uprising and National Liberation Movement in Serbia 1941) *passim* and Djilas, *Wartime*, pp. 91-114. See also Sergije M. Živanović, *Djeneral Mihailović i njegovo delo* (General Mihailović and His Work), III, *passim*.

10. *The Trial of Dragoljub-Draza Mihailović*, pp. 110-112.

11. Marjanović, *Ustanak i narodnooslobodilački pokret u srbiji 1941*, p. 247.

12. Tito had foreseen a world war would erupt that would lead to the occupation of Yugoslavia and the ultimate triumph of the communists. They had "to seize power and seize it in such a way that the bourgeoisie would never again regain it." There was to be no bourgeois revolution he told a central committee meeting, but must lead to the dictatorship of the proletariat. Fitzroy Maclean, *Tito* (N.Y., 1957), p. 93f. quoting Vladimir Dedijer, *Josip Broz Tito, prilozi za biografia* (Belgrade, 1953), p. 275.

13. Djilas denies his responsibility for the reprisals against enemies carried out in Montenegro during the 1941 uprising and for "errors" of strategy by the Montenegrin party leadership which he presided over. For his explanations see Djilas, *Wartime*, p. 79ff. Djilas also writes that "in 1943 Kardelj let slip the remark that grave "sectarian errors" had been made in Serbia in 1941" which he thought to have meant the too narrow communist form the movement had taken there in both the exclusively communist leadership and organization and the use of symbols (red star, clenched fist salute, etc.), *Ibid.*, 99.

14. According to one source the total foreign investment in private corporations in Yugoslavia was 33 per cent, which is much higher if spare parts, production methods and equipment is considered. At the end of 1937 total foreign held share capital came to 44 per cent. See Jozo Tomasevich, "Foreign Economic Relations," in *Yugoslavia* (ed. Robert J. Kerner)(Berkeley and Los Angeles, 1949), pp. 188,193.

15. When the Italians questioned the Germans on their political intentions in the Yugoslav area, Ribbentrop sent a memo declaring that "in all questions of the Mediterranean the policy of the Axis is determined in Rome and that Germany would never conduct a policy independent of Italy's." *Unpublished German Foreign Office Documents*, Berlin, memo, March 21, 1939 (Hereafter *UGFOD*).

16. The conflict between western capitalist interests in the southeast is described in Živko Avramovski, "Sukob interesa Veliki Britanije i Nemacka na Balkanu," (The Clash of British and German Interests

in the Balkans), *Istorija XX veka* (Belgrade, 1959), 2, pp. 5-158. The Italian candidly viewed a war between the Anglo-French "conservative, plutocratic" powers and the German-Italian "populous and poor" powers as inevitable." See *I documenti diplomatici italiani*, VII, 12, Doc. 59. For a recent study on German ambitions in this area see Hans-Jürgen Schröder, "Südosteuropa als 'Informal Empire' Deutschlands 1933-1939: Das Beispiel Jugoslawien," *Jahrbücher fur Geschichte Osteuropas* (1975), pp. 70-96.

17. Milovan Djilas, *Conversations with Stalin* (N.Y., 1962), p. 114. See also Djilas, *Wartime*, p. 438.

18. Agram, October 1, 1941, Glaise to OKW, GGAF 308/41.

19. Maclean, *Tito*, p. 84.

20. Agram, November 16, 1941, Glaise to OKW, GGAF 377/41.

21. Agram, October 1, 1941, Glaise to OKW, GGAF 309/41.

22. Agram, December 6, 1941, Glaise to OKW, GGAF 3062/41.

23. On the controversial March 1941 coup see the recent article by David A.T. Stafford, "SOE and British Involvement in the Belgrade Coup d'Etat of March 1941," *Slavic Review*, September 1977, Vol. 36, No. 3.

24. *Ibid.*, p. 413, *n*.52.

25. For Maček's account of his wartime imprisonment see Vladko Maček, *In the Struggle for Freedom* (Penn. State Univ., 1957).

26. It should also be mentioned that both the četniks and partisans engaged in what are described as "parallel actions." Sometimes the partisans joined the Germans against the četniks and at times the nationalists joined the Germans or Italians against the partisans. One such action in which the Second Proletariat Brigade moved from Montenegro to East Bosnia and joined the Germans, Ustasha and Croatian army forces against the numerically strong East Bosnian nationalists. A German *Lagebericht* states: "Between the Croatian Communists, Ustasha and the Proletariat Brigade thrusting from parts of Montenegro a kind of agreement seems to have been struck according to which these groups will not fight one another." German intelligence also reported that "Ustasha units and partisans fighting together against Dangić (the East Bosnian nationalist leader)." German Military Commander in Serbia to WB Südost, *Lagebericht* for the period March-April 1942. Partially as a result the large East Bosnian nationalist group was liquidated by the Germans. However, četnik collaboration with the enemy was apparently carried out much more frequently. Accounts of this are contained in *OSS Documents*, R & N No. 1662, dated June 15, 1944, 81 pages of captured četnik documents given the Americans by partisan representatives describing co-operation by Radić, Djuić, Vuketić and various Bosnian četnik leaders with the Ustasha and Domobrani.

27. Von Glaise Horstenau laid the blame for the spread of the partisan movement inside Croatia at the door of the Ustasha: "I cannot conceal that I ascribe to the Ustasha's uncontrolled emergence a greater share in the spread of the uprising than does the minister

(Siegfried Kasche, the pro-Ustasha German representative in Zagreb). That relates also to the uprising in the Herzegovina which occurred even before the Russian war." Agram, Glaise to OKW, Feb. 10, 1942, GGAF 50/42. However Djilas believes that even if the massacres of the Serbs in the Croatian state had not taken place the insurrection against the occupier would have occurred anyway sooner or later by the people, and would have been impossible to prevent.

28. Dedijer, *Dnevnik*, I, p. 27. Djilas admits that there had been no call for a revolution against the Axis occupiers until the German attack on the USSR in June 1941 but that it would have occurred even without Moscow's directive. "The party was undoubtedly devoted to Moscow and beyond its direct control. The attack on the USSR, and the reign of terror by the occupation forces and domestic fascists would have led them to take up arms even without the Moscow directives." Djilas, *Wartime*, p. 5.

29. Dedijer notes: "From the beginning the Party was able to count on its membership. The communists were really the motor force of the National Liberation struggle." *Ibid.*, p. 29. Djilas puts the number at about 3,000 party members in western Serbia in 1941. Djilas, *Wartime*, p. 100.

30. Maclean, *Tito*, p. 100ff.

31. *UGFOD*, Belgrade, Benzler to Auswärtiges Amt, Berlin, August 8, 1941.

32. This strategy was also suggested during the Viet Nam war by the American General Gavin who proposed that the American forces withdraw to the coastal enclaves and abandon the hinterland to the Viet Cong guerrillas.

I
Political and Military Situation After Balkan Campaign

1. Fuehrer Directive No. 31 dated June 9, 1941.

2. From the report on conditions by Corps Command LXV.

3. Order of Corps Command LXV dated 14 July 1941 on the provision of divisions of the 15th Wave with captured heavy weapons and the formation of reconnaissance sections.

II
The Beginning of the Insurgent Movement in Serbia and Croatia

1. Corps Command LXV Ia No. 373/41 secret dated 16.7.41.

III
The Suppression of the Revolt in Serbia

1. Commander in Serbia. Diary No. 731/41 secret. Reasons for the creation of new Serbian government, Nedić.

2. Ia No. 2015/41 secret of 8. September 1941.

3. Ia No. 1892/41 top secret of 10 September 1941.

4. Ia No. 1891/41 top secret of 11 September 1941.

5. Ia No. 1913/41 top secret of 13 September 1941.

6. Commander Serbia. 1923/41 top secret of 15/9/41.

7. Wehrmacht Commander Southeast Ia. No. 1923/41 top secret of 15/9/41.

8. The German General in Zagreb to the Wehrmacht Commander Southeast, No. 291/41 top secret of 19/9/41.

9. Wehrmacht Commander Southeast Ia. No. 1946/41 top secret of 17.9.1941.

10. OKW/WFst. Dept. National Defense. (1 Op) 441.538/41 top secret of 17.9.41. Wehrmacht Commander Southeast Ia.No. 1953. 1954. 1959/41 top secret of 18 September 1941.

11. Plenipotentiary Commanding General in Serbia Ic 2417/41 secret of 22.9.41.

12. The Chief of the General Staff of the Wehrmacht Commander Southeast. Ia. No. 2336/41 top secret of 6.10.41.

13. Plenipotentiary Commanding General in Serbia Ia No. 931/41 top secret of 30.10.41.

14. The regiment had finished its mopping up operations south of Belgrade on October 31.

15. From the 10th to the 20th of November the number of insurgents who appeared in battle was estimated at 513, the number of hostages shot, as 305.

16. From the speech of the Chief (of Staff) on 17.11.41.

17. The General Staff Chief of the LXV Corps Command, Colonel Kewisch, reported personally on this incident to General of Engineers Kuntze, in the presence of Brigadier General Foertsch.

18. The holding back of Mihailovic' in the fight against the German Wehrmacht, and his offer to the Plen. Commdg. General in Serbia to take part pn the side of the German units against the Communists, was probably to be traced back to the fact that Mihailović had not finished building up his forces and feared, that in a fight with German troops, he might be forced out of his provisioning territories.

19. On the 11.20 the Plen. Comm. Gen. in Serbia announced as his intention "the commitment of the 342nd Infantry Division from the Lubovjia region (Drina valley) and Valjevo, and of the 113th Infantry Division from Kragujevac and Kraljevo for the destruction of the enemy in the Western Morava valley and in Užice."—Plen. Commdg. Gen. in Serbia Ia. No. 988/41 top secret.

20. It concerned the reinforced protection of the copper mines at Bor, the lead and tin mines at Trepca, the antimony works at Krupanje and Ivanjich (antimony work at Zajecar, southeast of Loznica), the magnesium mines near Užice, the pyrite mines near Dl. Milanovac and the coal mines of eastern Serbia, as well as the reinforced security of the transport lines to and from these mines.

21. From the speeches of the Chief (of Staff) on November 14 and 17, 1941. The great significance of Old Serbia and Bosnia for the conduct of the war was in no way disregarded by the Wehrmacht Commander Southeast. But there must be an understanding of motives if he gave military necessities priority over industrial demands. A military attack is the most direct way to attain the suppression of the insurgent movement, and the restoration of peace and order in the country. Industry could be helped quickly and effectively even if the industrially important points had to be sacrificed temporarily.

An armed and equipped "Factory Guard", with a maximum strength of 5,000 men was organized from emigrant Russians in Serbia for the reinforced protection of industrial plants.

22. Plen. Commdg. Gen. in Serbia. Ia. No. 1024/42 top secret of 11.30.41.

23. Plen. Commdg. Gen. in Serbia Ia. No. 339/41 top secret of 16.12.

IV
The Flaring Up of the Band War in Bosnia

1. General Glaise-Horstenau reported this in a situation report to Wehrmacht Commander Southeast (German General in Zagreb Ia. No. 419/41 top secret.

2. German General in Zagreb. No. 346/41 top secret of 6.10.41.

3. The German General in Zagreb Ia. No. 291/41 top secret of 9.19.41.

4. The German General in Zagreb Ia. No. 377/41 and 419/41 top secret.

5. German General in Zagreb Ia. 419/41 top secret.

6. German General in Zagreb, Ia. No. 419/41.

7. Chief of OKW/WFSt? Dept. Home Defense, I. Ops. No. 164/41 top secret of 12.16.41.

8. German General with the HQ of the Italian Armed Forces Ia. 3767/42 top secret of 12/19/41.

9. German General in Zagreb Ia No. 410/41 top secret of 12/16/41.

10. Wehrmacht Commander Southeast, Ia. No. 0316/41 top secret of 12/20/41.

11. The German General in Zagreb, Ia. No. 418/41 top secret of 12/22/41.

12. The German General in Zagreb, Ia. No. 411/41 top secret.

13. German General in Zagreb, Ia. No. 420/41 top secret.

14. Wehrmacht Commander Southeast, Ia No. 2634/41 top secret.

V
Combatting the Revolt in Bosnia

1. Wehrmacht Commander Southeast, Ia/Ic No. 35/42, 1.5.42.

2. Wehrmacht Commander Southeast, Ia/Ic 99/42 top secret of 1.21.42.

3. German General in Zagreb, No. 21/42 top secret of 1/26.

4. Wehrmacht Commander Southeast, Ia. No. 342/42 top secret.

5. Plenipotentiary Commanding General in Serbia, Ia. No. 431/42 secret of 2.6.42.

6. Plenipotentiary Commanding General in Serbia, Ia. No. secret of 2/5/42.

7. Wehrmacht Commander Southeast Ia/Ic No. 483/42 top secret of 2/13/42.

8. From a report of the Plenipotentiary Commanding General in Serbia.

9. German General in Zagreb. 21/42 top secret of 21.1.42.

10. Wehrmacht Commander Southeast, Ia. No. 010/42 top secret of 2.5.42.

11. Wehrmacht Commander Southeast Ia. No. 500/42 top secret.

VI
The Abbazia Discussions and the Resulting Joint Operations

1. Chief OKW/WESt Ops. No, 00555/42 top secret of 2.4.42.

2. Report of the German Liaison Staff with the Italian Second Army No. 153/42 top secret of 1/26/42.

3. Teletype of the OKW/WFSt Ops. No. 00732/42 top secret of 2/23/42 to Wehrmacht Commander Southeast (Wehrmacht Commander Southeast Ia. No. 569/42 top secret of 2.24.42).

4. OKW/WFSt Ops (H) No. 00744/42 top secret of 2/24/42 (Wehrmacht Commander Southeast Ia. No. 568/42 top secret of 2.23.42).

5. Telegram Wehrmacht Commander Southeast Ia. No. 5000/42 top secret to OKW/WFSt and to OKH/Gen. StdH-Ops Dept.

6. Chief OKW/WFSt Ops. No. 00719/42 top secret of 2/28.

7. Wehrmacht Commander Southeast Ia. No. 05001/42 top secret of 3/4/42.

8. Wehrmacht Commander Southeast, Ia. No. 648/42 top secret of 3.6.42.

9. OKW/Foreign Office/Counter Intelligence. No. 429/42 top secret—Ic. of 3.18.42 as well as Twelfth Army Ia. No. 842/42 to secret of 2.26.42.

10. The German General in Zagreb to the Wehrmacht Commander Southeast. Wehrmacht Commander Southeast Ia. No. 115/42 top secret of 3.25.42 and Wehrmacht Commander Southeast Ia. No. 816/42 top secret of 3.26.42.

11. As from the 3.1.42 the previous positions "Plenipotentiary Commanding General in Serbia", "the LXV Corps Command for

Special Employment", and "the Commander in Serbia" were concentrated in one single office, the "Commanding General and Commander in Serbia." The current tasks of the Commanding General
and Commander in Serbia,(General of Artillery Bader) were carried
out by his chief of staff, General Staff Colonel Kewisch, during the
former's absence in Bosnia.

12. Wehrmacht Commander Southeast Ia. No. 733/42 top secret
of 3.17 and Ia. No. 968/42 secret of 3.16.42.

13. Combat Group Bader Ia. No. 2/42 top secret and Wehrmacht
Commander Southeast Ia. No. 764/42 top secret.

14. The following were present at the discussions: General of the
Army Roatta, Commander in Chief of the Italian Second Army,
General of Artillery Bader, Commander of the Combat Group Bader,
Major General Laxa, Chief of the General Staff of the Croatian Wehr-
macht, for the Germans, in addition to Lt. Colonel Pfafferott Chief
of Staff of Combat Group Bader, Colonel Rohrbach, Liaison Officer
with the Italian Second Army, Lt. Col. Graf Spee as representative
of the German General in Zagreb. For the Italians, Corps General
Robboti, Commanding General of the Italian XL Infantry Corps,
Brigadier General Blaslo, Chief of Staff of the Italian Second Army,
Lt. Colonel Peterzani, Chief of the Italian XI Infantry Corps.

15. In paragraph 10 of the protocol it was agreed that no negotiations should be taken up with the insurgents, either with the Četniks
or with the Communists.

16. Combat Group Bader Ia. No. 101/42 top secret of 3/29.

17. Combat Group Bader Ia. 102/42 top secret of 3.29.42.

18. Combat Group Bader Ia No. 102/42 top secret, radio message
of 3/29-Wehrmacht Commander Southeast Ia. No. 845/42 top secret.

19. Wehrmacht Commander Southeast 666/42 top secret of 4/1/42.

20. Wehrmacht Commander Southeast Ia. No. 845/42 top secret.

21. Wehrmacht Commander Southeast Ia. No. 869/42 top secret
of 4.3.42.

22. Wehrmacht Commander Southeast Ia. No. 878/42 top secret
of 3/4/42.

23. OKW/WFSt/Ops. No. 001165/42 top secret of 4/4. Wehrmacht Commander Southeast Ia. No. 886/42 top secret.

24. The German General with the Headquarters of the Italian
Wehrmacht Ia. No. 845/42 top secret of 4/6. Wehrmacht Commander
Southeast Ia. No. 904/42 top secret.

25. The leader of the Serb insurgents in East Bosnia, Dangic, who
at the beginning of April was still in Belgrade, (pages 126, 127) was
taken prisoner by German units on April 13 near Rogatica on the
Drina and sent to a detention camp in the Reich.

26. German Liaison Officer with the Italian Second Army, 0785/
42 of 4.7.42.

27. Operational staff of the CombatGroup Bader Ia. No. 732/42
top secret of 4.5.42.

28. Wehrmacht Commander Southeast Ia. No. 992/42 top secret and 1007/42 top secret of 4.16.42.

29. German General in Rome Ia. No. 974/42 top secret of 4.18.42-Wehrmacht Commander Southeast Ia. No. 1010/42 top secret of 4.10.42.

30. Combat Group Bader Ia. No. 311/42 secret of 4.20.42 Wehrmacht Commander Southeast Ia. No. 1432/42 secret of 4.20.42.

31. Combat Group Bader Ia. No. 319/42 secret of 20.4.41 (Wehrmacht Commander Southeast Ia. No. 1492/42 secret of 4.23.42.

32. Combat Group Bader Ia. No. 331/42 secret—(Wehrmacht Commander Southeast Ia. No. 1452/42 secret of 4.21.42).

33. Commanding General and Commander in Serbia Ia. No. 255/42 top secret and 256/42 top secret of 5.23 and Ia. No. 363/42 top secret of 5.26 (Wehrmacht Commander Southeast Ia. No. 1295/42 top secret and 1296/42 top secret of 5.28.42).

34. German General in Zagreb Ia. No. 83/42 top secret of 5.23 (Wehrmacht Commander Southeast Ia. No. 1267/42 top secret of 5.24.42).

35. Losses in the period from 7-23.6.42
   Germans: Dead 19, wounded, 31, missing 6
   Croatians: Dead 200, wounded 250, missing 169
   Insurgents: Dead 1,748, wounded 15, prisoners 713, shot in reprisal, 275

36. Wehrmacht Commander Southeast. Telegram to the OKW Ia. No. 1236/42 and 1238/42 top secret of 5.20.42.

37. Wehrmacht Commander Southeast Ia. No. 1599/42 top secret of 7.2.42.

38. Losses of the insurgents from 6.24-7.8: Dead: 4,963, wounded, 150, prisoners, 6,641, shot in reprisal: 346.

39. Wehrmacht Commander Southeast Ia. No. 1683/42 top secret of 7.12.42.

40. Commanding General and Commander in Serbia Ia. No. 4098/42 of 7.17.42.

41. Operational staff of the Combat Group West Bosnia No. 1749/42 of 7.27.42.

42. Wehrmacht Commander Southeast Ia. No. 2014/42 secret of 8.6.42.

43. Since July 20, General Staff Colonel Schipp von Pranitz had conducted the affairs of the leader of the operational department Ia in place of General Staff Colonel Macher who had been posted to the East front as Chief of Staff of a Corps.

EAST EUROPEAN MONOGRAPHS

The *East European Monographs* comprise scholarly books on the history and civilization of Eastern Europe. They are published by the *East European Quarterly* in the belief that these studies contribute substantially to the knowledge of the area and serve to stimulate scholarship and research.

1. *Political Ideas and the Enlightenment in the Romanian Principalities, 1750–1831.* By Vlad Georgescu. 1971.
2. *America, Italy and the Birth of Yugoslavia, 1917–1919.* By Dragan R. Zivojinovic. 1972.
3. *Jewish Nobles and Geniuses in Modern Hungary.* By William O. McCagg, Jr. 1972.
4. *Mixail Soloxov in Yugoslavia: Reception and Literary Impact.* By Robert F. Price. 1973.
5. *The Historical and National Thought of Nicolae Iorga.* By William O. Oldson. 1973.
6. *Guide to Polish Libraries and Archives.* By Richard C. Lewanski. 1974.
7. *Vienna Broadcasts to Slovakia, 1938–1939: A Case Study in Subversion.* By Henry Delfiner. 1974.
8. *The 1917 Revolution in Latvia.* By Andrew Ezergailis. 1974.
9. *The Ukraine in the United Nations Organization: A Study in Soviet Foreign Policy. 1944–1950.* By Konstantin Sawczuk. 1975.
10. *The Bosnian Church: A New Interpretation.* By John V. A. Fine, Jr., 1975.
11. *Intellectual and Social Developments in the Habsburg Empire from Maria Theresa to World War I.* Edited by Stanley B. Winters and Joseph Held. 1975.
12. *Ljudevit Gaj and the Illyrian Movement.* By Elinor Murray Despalatovic. 1975.
13. *Tolerance and Movements of Religious Dissent in Eastern Europe.* Edited by Bela K. Kiraly. 1975.
14. *The Parish Republic: Hlinka's Slovak People's Party, 1939–1945.* By Yeshayahu Jelinek. 1976.
15. *The Russian Annexation of Bessarabia, 1774–1828.* By George F. Jewsbury. 1976.
16. *Modern Hungarian Historiography.* By Steven Bela Vardy. 1976.
17. *Values and Community in Multi-National Yugoslavia.* By Gary K. Bertsch. 1976.
18. *The Greek Socialist Movement and the First World War: the Road to Unity.* By George B. Leon. 1976.
19. *The Radical Left in the Hungarian Revolution of 1848.* By Laszlo Deme. 1976.

20. *Hungary between Wilson and Lenin: The Hungarian Revolution of 1918–1919 and the Big Three.* By Peter Pastor. 1976.

21. *The Crises of France's East-Central European Diplomacy, 1933–1938.* By Anthony J. Komjathy. 1976.

22. *Polish Politics and National Reform, 1775–1788.* By Daniel Stone. 1976.

23. *The Habsburg Empire in World War I.* Robert A. Kann, Bela K. Kiraly, and Paula S. Fichtner, eds. 1977.

24. *The Slovenes and Yugoslavism, 1890–1914.* By Carole Rogel. 1977.

25. *German-Hungarian Relations and the Swabian Problem.* By Thomas Spira. 1977.

26. *The Metamorphosis of a Social Class in Hungary During the Reign of Young Franz Joseph.* By Peter I. Hidas. 1977.

27. *Tax Reform in Eighteenth Century Lombardy.* By Daniel M. Klang. 1977.

28. *Tradition versus Revolution: Russia and the Balkans in 1917.* By Robert H. Johnston. 1977.

29. *Winter into Spring: The Czechoslovak Press and the Reform Movement 1963–1968.* By Frank L. Kaplan. 1977.

30. *The Catholic Church and the Soviet Government, 1939–1949.* By Dennis J. Dunn. 1977.

31. *The Hungarian Labor Service System, 1939–1945.* By Randolph L. Braham. 1977.

32. *Consciousness and History: Nationalist Critics of Greek Society 1897–1914.* By Gerasimos Augustinos. 1977.

33. *Emigration in Polish Social and Political Thought, 1870–1914.* By Benjamin P. Murdzek. 1977.

34. *Serbian Poetry and Milutin Bojic.* By Mihailo Dordevic. 1977.

35. *The Baranya Dispute: Diplomacy in the Vortex of Ideologies, 1918–1921.* By Leslie C. Tihany. 1978.

36. *The United States in Prague, 1945–1948.* By Walter Ullmann. 1978.

37. *Rush to the Alps: The Evolution of Vacationing in Switzerland.* By Paul P. Bernard. 1978.

38. *Transportation in Eastern Europe: Empirical Findings.* By Bogdan Mieczkowski. 1978.

39. *The Polish Underground State: A Guide to the Underground, 1939–1945.* By Stefan Korbonski. 1978.

40. *The Hungarian Revolution of 1956 in Retrospect.* Edited by Bela K. Kiraly and Paul Jonas. 1978.

41. *Boleslaw Limanowski (1835–1935): A Study in Socialism and Nationalism.* By Kazimiera Janina Cottam. 1978.

42. *The Lingering Shadow of Nazism: The Austrian Independent Party Movement Since 1945.* By Max E. Riedlsperger. 1978.

43. *The Catholic Church, Dissent and Nationality in Soviet Lithuania.* By V. Stanley Vardys. 1978.

44. *The Development of Parliamentary Government in Serbia.* By Alex N. Dragnich. 1978.

45. *Divide and Conquer: German Efforts to Conclude a Separate Peace, 1914–1918.* By L. L. Farrar, Jr. 1978.
46. *The Prague Slav Congress of 1848.* By Lawrence D. Orton. 1978.
47. *The Nobility and the Making of the Hussite Revolution.* By John M. Klassen. 1978.
48. *The Cultural Limits of Revolutionary Politics: Change and Continuity in Socialist Czechoslovakia.* By David W. Paul. 1979.
49. *On the Border of War and Peace: Polish Intelligence and Diplomacy in 1937-1939 and the Origins of the Ultra Secret.* By Richard A. Woytak. 1979.
50. *Bear and Foxes: The International Relations of the East European States 1965-1969.* By Ronald Haly Linden. 1979.
51. *Czechoslovakia: The Heritage of Ages Past.* Edited by Ivan Volgyes and Hans Brisch. 1979.
52. *Prime Minister Gyula Andrássy's Influence on Habsburg Foreign Policy.* By János Decsy. 1979.
53. *Citizens for the Fatherland: Education, Educators, and Pedagogical Ideals in Eighteenth Century Russia.* By J. L. Black. 1979.
54. *A History of the "Proletariat": The Emergence of Marxism in the Kingdom of Poland, 1870-1887.* By Norman M. Naimark. 1979.
55. *The Slovak Autonomy Movement, 1935-1939: A Study in Unrelenting Nationalism.* By Dorothea H. El Mallakh. 1979.
56. *Diplomat in Exile: Francis Pulszky's Political Activities in England, 1849-1860.* By Thomas Kabdebo. 1979.
57. *The German Struggle Against the Yugoslav Guerrillas in World War II: German Counter-Insurgency in Yugoslavia, 1941-1943.* By Paul N. Hehn. 1979.
58. *The Emergence of the Romanian National State.* By Gerald J. Bobango. 1979.
59. *Stewards of the Land: The American Farm School and Modern Greece.* By Brenda L. Marder. 1979.